This book provides an important and interesting insight into the hospitality and tourism sectors. The focus on the institutional theory provides a refreshing view on how policy and governance can influence the rules of the game of the hospitality and tourism industry. Definitely a compulsory resource for students and novice researchers in various social science disciplines.

Jose Huesca Dorantes, *University of Auckland Business School,*
New Zealand

While the importance of the institutional environment in understanding tourism is well recognized, a comprehensive review of recent advances in institutional theory from neighbouring disciplines and their application to tourism studies is missing. This book provides a thorough review of institutional perspectives in organisational sociology, economics, political science, and international business, and proposes an integrative framework with a rich discussion on how the different elements of institutional analysis can be applied to better understand tourism organisations. In addition, the book provides an excellent reflection on the methodological challenges of "doing" institutional analysis. As such, this book will be of great value for students of tourism and in advancing institutional analysis in tourism studies.

Ziad Elsahn, *University of Northumbria, UK*

This book must be welcomed as pioneer comprehensive research on the application of institutional theory to tourism and hospitality. Tourism and hospitality businesses are able to develop and flourish by understanding the institutional environment they operate in. This book is invaluable for researchers and university students.

Sergei Polbitsyn, *Ural Federal University, Russia*

Institutional Theory in Tourism and Hospitality

Institutions are fundamental aspects for driving tourism and hospitality globally. They are the socio-economic "rules of the game" that serve to shape and constrain human and organisational interactions. This book is the first of its kind to provide a comprehensive overview of institutional theory in a tourism and hospitality context.

The complexity and multiple scaled nature of the institutional environment plays a crucial role in the development and formation of tourism destinations, attractions, organisations, and businesses, as well as influencing the activities of individuals. Institutional theory therefore provides a means to understand the complexity and processes of change at different scales of analysis and provides insights into the organisational and political basis of tourism policy development and implementation. Chapters introduce and expand on institutional analysis in tourism and hospitality, institutional theory in the social sciences, methodological issues, and future directions in institutional analysis in tourism and hospitality, making use of case studies throughout.

This book will appeal to students of tourism, hospitality, leisure, and events, as well as other social science disciplines. Providing a comprehensive overview of and guide to the application of institutional theory, this book will serve as a complete reference to institutional theory in a tourism and hospitality setting for years to come.

Anna Earl is a Lecturer in Management at the University of Canterbury, New Zealand. Her main research interests include the application of institutional theory to various disciplines, the relationship between government and multi-national enterprises in Russia and other emerging economies, and the internationalisation processes of multi-national enterprises. She is also interested in methodological issues related to conducting research in emerging and developed economies.

C. Michael Hall is a Professor in the Department of Management, Marketing, and Entrepreneurship at the University of Canterbury, New Zealand; Docent in Geography, University of Oulu, Finland; a Visiting Professor in Tourism at Linnaeus University, Kalmar, Sweden; and a Guest Professor in the Department of Service Management and Service Studies, Lund University, Helsingborg, Sweden. He has written widely on tourism, regional development, policy, heritage, food, and global environmental change.

Routledge Focus on Tourism and Hospitality Research

Routledge Focus on Tourism and Hospitality Research presents small books on big topics and how they intersect with the world of tourism and hospitality research. The idea is to fill the gap between journal article and book. This new short-form series offers both established and early-career academics the flexibility to publish cutting-edge commentary on the latest research methodologies, applied research, theory construction, literature reviews and skills such as how to get published and how to write a proposal related to tourism and hospitality in a succinct way.

City Integration and Tourism Development in the Greater Bay Area, China
Jian Ming Luo and Chi Fung Lam

Institutional Theory in Tourism and Hospitality
Anna Earl and C. Michael Hall

For more information about this series, please visit: www.routledge.com/Routledge-Focus-on-Tourism-and-Hospitality-Research/book-series/FTHR

Institutional Theory in Tourism and Hospitality

Anna Earl and C. Michael Hall

Routledge
Taylor & Francis Group

LONDON AND NEW YORK

First published 2021
by Routledge
2 Park Square, Milton Park, Abingdon, Oxon OX14 4RN

and by Routledge
605 Third Avenue, New York, NY 10158

Routledge is an imprint of the Taylor & Francis Group, an informa business

British Library Cataloguing-in-Publication Data
A catalogue record for this book is available from the British Library

Library of Congress Cataloging-in-Publication Data
Names: Earl, Anna, author. | Hall, C. Michael, author.
Title: Institutional theory in tourism and hospitality/
Anna Earl and C. Michael Hall.
Description: Abingdon, Oxon; New York, NY: Routledge, 2021. |
Series: Routledge focus on tourism and hospitality |
Includes bibliographical references and index.
Identifiers: LCCN 2021002099 (print) | LCCN 2021002100 (ebook)
Subjects: LCSH: Tourism–Management. |
Hospitality industry–Management.
Classification: LCC G155.A1 E22 2021 (print) |
LCC G155.A1 (ebook) | DDC 910.68–dc23
LC record available at https://lccn.loc.gov/2021002099
LC ebook record available at https://lccn.loc.gov/2021002100

ISBN: 978-0-367-50775-6 (hbk)
ISBN: 978-0-367-50776-3 (pbk)
ISBN: 978-1-003-05120-6 (ebk)

Typeset in Times New Roman
by Deanta Global Publishing Services, Chennai, India

Anna would like to dedicate this book to her late father, Alexander Zubkovsky

Michael would like to dedicate it to the memory of JC who always knew a good theory when he saw one, and to Ron James and John Selwood who always liked a glass of wine with theirs

Contents

Figures

Tables

Boxes and cases

Preface and acknowledgements

Institutions are an essential part of society, the economy, and politics. Both our research and personal lives are greatly affected by them. The capacity to travel, as illustrated only too well in the pandemic year of 2020, is deeply affected by rules and regulations, while simultaneously tourism and hospitality businesses and organisations have had to respond to their new institutional environment. This work emerged out of our previous research on institutions and their effects and a realisation that despite the increased attention being given to their role in tourism and wider social science research there was not a ready introduction for students of tourism to this important area of research. We hope therefore that this introductory volume will help fill this gap.

For Anna, no one has been a greater inspiration and motivation to her than her family and colleagues. She would like to thank her late father, who has always encouraged to her to question everything and investigate how businesses operate in complex institutional environments. She would like to thank her mother for always providing her with facts on what reality is, in challenging business contexts. Most importantly, She would like to thank her husband, Rob, for looking after the family and inspiring her to pursue an academic career. She would also like to thank her colleagues Ziad Elsahn, Sanna Malinen, Russell Wordsworth, Sarah Wright, Girish Prayag, Sussie Morrish, Christina Stringer, Snejina Michailova, Dana Ott, Jose Huesca Dorantes, Sergey Polbitsyn, Sara McGaughey, Matt Raskovic, and Smita Paul for their endless support, encouragement, and feedback.

Michael would like to specifically thank a number of colleagues with whom he has undertaken related conversations and research over the years. In particular, thanks go to Bailey Adie, Alberto Amore, Paul Ballantine, Dorothee Bohn, Chris Chen, Tim Coles, Hervé Corvellec, David Duval, Stefan Gössling, Martin Gren, Dikte Grønvold, Johan Hultman, Tyron Love, Dieter Müller, Jan-Henrik Nilsson, Yuri Oh, Girish Prayag, Jarkko Saarinen, Anna Dóra Sæþórsdóttir, Dan Scott, Siamak Seyfi, Allan Williams,

Kimberley Wood, and Maria José Zapata Campos for their thoughts, as well as for the stimulation of Agnes Obel, Ann Brun, Beirut, Paul Buchanan, Bill Callahan, Nick Cave, Bruce Cockburn, Ebba Fosberg, Mark Hollis, Margaret Glaspy, Aimee Mann, Larkin Poe, Vinnie Reilly, Henry Rollins, Matthew Sweet, Emma Swift, TISM, Henry Wagon, and *The Guardian*, BBC6, JJ, and KCRW – for making the world much less confining. Special mention must also be given to the Malmö Saluhall; Balck, Packhuset, and Postgarten in Kalmar; and Nicole Aignier and the Hotel Grüner Baum in Merzhausen. Finally, and most importantly, Michael would like to thank the Js and the Cs who stay at home and mind the farm.

We also wish to gratefully acknowledge the help and support of Jody Cowper for her indispensable proofreading and editing. Finally, we would both like to thank Emma Travis, Lydia Kessell, and all at Routledge for their continuing support.

Abbreviations

CSR	Corporate Social Responsibility
FAO	Food and Agriculture Organisation of the United Nations
MNE	Multi-national enterprises
NGO	Non-government organisation
OECD	Organisation for Economic Cooperation and Development
UNDP	UN Development Program
UNEP	UN Environmental Program
UNWTO	UN World Tourism Organization
WHO	World Health Organization
WTO	World Trade Organization
WTTC	World Travel & Tourism Council

1 Institutional analysis and tourism

An introduction

Introduction

Institutions are a fundamental building block of society and of its study. Although there is no single agreed definition, an institution represents a social order or pattern that has attained a certain state and which helps establish the "rules of the game" (Hotimsky et al., 2006) by which organisations and individuals act and the bases for compliance and legitimacy of those organisations (North, 1990). Therefore, given their importance for social, economic, and political order, it is perhaps not surprising that institutions, broadly conceived, are a central idea of the social sciences as well as ideas regarding society, organisations, and how and to what purpose they are governed and act. Table 1.1 illustrates some of these ideas with reference to some of the key elements of Scott's (2014) three pillars model of institutions. However, it is important to recognise that this three pillars approach, although highly influential and useful illustratively, has also been substantially criticised as being too reductionist (Hirsch & Lounsbury, 1997, 2015) reflecting that institutions are an essentially contested concept and their study remains open.

Institutions have long been the subject of political, economic, and social scientific thought (Scott, 2014). However, over the past 50 or so years, the study of institutions has expanded – what is widely referred to as new institutionalism or neoinstitutionalism (March & Olsen, 1984) – to become a particular field of knowledge in geography, management, organisational studies, sociology, and the wider social sciences, which constitutes what is generally referred to as institutional theory (Meyer & Rowan, 1977; Suchman, 1995; Tolbert & Zucker, 1999; Weerakkody et al., 2009; Kauppi, 2013; Munir, 2015). Elements of institutional analysis were adopted in tourism and hospitality studies in the 1990s, particularly with respect to the importance of organisational networks and collaboration (Selin, 1994; Palmer, 1996; Bramwell & Lane, 2000a; Casanueva et al., 2016) amid the

Table 1.1 Three elements of institutions

	Regulative	Social-Normative	Cultural-Cognitive
Basis of compliance	Expedience	Social obligation	Taken-for-grantedness, shared understanding
Basis of order	Regulative rules	Obligations and expectations	Constitutive schema, social practices
Mechanisms	Coercive – Formal and informal pressures such as government regulations and/or local culture	Normative – Arising from professionalisation, particularly of functional fields	Mimetic – Arising from uncertainty, organisations will imitate other organisations that appear successful or legitimate
Logic	Instrumentality	Appropriateness	Orthodoxy
indicators	Rules, laws, regulations, sanctions	Certification, accreditation, membership	Common beliefs, shared logics of action, isomorphism
Basis of legitimacy	Legally sanctioned	Morally governed, self-regulation	Comprehensible, recognisable, culturally supported

Source: After Scott, 2014; DiMaggio & Powell, 1983.

hollowing of the state (Hall, 1999; Bramwell & Lane, 2000b). In more recent years, the direct use of institutional theory in tourism and hospitality studies has grown substantially (Lavandoski et al., 2014), and has been used to explain phenomena including, among others, social entrepreneurship (McCarthy, 2012), reproductive tourism (Yang, 2020), adaptation in environmental management (DeBoer et al., 2017; Mensah & Blankson, 2013; Ouyang et al., 2019; Zhu et al., 2013), corporate social responsibility reporting (De Grosbois, 2016), investment in experiential learning (Dicen et al., 2019), anti-smoking regulations (Simons et al., 2016), and the adoption of technology such as e-marketing (Gyau & Stringer, 2011). It is not yet clear as to whether tourism and hospitality organisations provide a 'special case' for institutional analysis, but it can be argued that they do have some particular features which arguably makes them more susceptible to changes in the institutional environment:

a) They are service organisations that are primarily focused on customers from outside of the immediate environment of the destination. This means that they are highly susceptible to any restrictions on voluntary mobility – which is the nature of tourism.
b) They tend to be highly networked organisations.
c) Organisations that are internationally focused and which are located in destinations are, like many international businesses, susceptible to changes in the institutional environments of both tourist generating region and the destination country.
d) The movement of people across borders is highly regulated at the national level.
e) Tourism has not historically been given much significance as a policy area despite its economic significance. This makes it highly susceptible to changes in other policy fields and regimes.
f) Travel may be susceptible to informal pressures arising from sociopolitical concerns regarding rights, justice, morality, religious mores, and the appropriateness of leisure behaviours.

All of the above reasons highlight the need for greater attention to be given to the analysis of the role of institutions in a tourism and hospitality context.

This book seeks to briefly introduce institutional theory to students of tourism and hospitality. It is important because institutional theory, and the debates within it, provide an extremely useful way for thinking about organisations and how they adapt and change to their environments, their trajectories, and how they are managed, particularly at a time when, more than ever, they may have to adapt in order to survive. In addition to thinking about commercial firms, institutional theory also helps in understanding

4 *Institutional analysis and tourism*

issues of collaboration, governance and policymaking, and implementation. This first chapter provides a very brief introduction to institutional theory and its significance, before the next chapter looks at the major elements of the theory. However, this chapter will first go on to discuss the importance of 'doing theory'.

The importance of theory and frameworks

Conceptual frameworks, such as images, models, and theories, are fundamental to the development of understanding public and private institutions and the relationships between them. For example, in his extremely influential work on images of organisations, Morgan (1986, p. 12) emphasised: "how many of our conventional ideas about organization and management build on a small number of taken-for-granted images, especially mechanical and biological ones". Similarly, Judge et al. (1995, p. 3) also noted that conceptual frameworks

> provide a language and frame of reference through which reality can be examined and lead theorists to ask questions that might not otherwise occur. The result, if successful, is new and fresh insights that other frameworks or perspectives might not have yielded.

One framework that is often used with respect to theory-building in the social sciences, which is used throughout this book, is typologies. A typology, an organised system of types, is an important means for looking at concept formation and measurement that are used widely in organisational and management studies, tourism studies, political science, and sociology (Hall, 2014) (see Table 1.1 for an example of a typology). In policy terms, typologies are used for both descriptive and explanatory purposes and can focus on variables related to causes, institutions, and/or outcomes (Collier et al., 2008). Typologies play an important role as instruments in developing more general insights into the ways in which key concepts and ideas can be framed so as to facilitate comparative studies and map empirical and theoretical change, and, although usually associated with qualitative research, can also contribute to the quantitative analysis of categorical variables (Collier et al., 2008).

By exploring different conceptual frameworks and images, it is possible to identify the ways in which empirical reality and theoretical models of that reality interact and how theory influences how the world is analysed, understood, and acted upon (Hall, 2014). In institutional and public policy terms, this notion is well illustrated by Pressman and Wildavsky's (1973, p. xv) insight that "policies imply theories". Majone (1980, 1981) also understood policies as well as the organisations and institutions from which they are often derived as theories in terms of their development in a quasi-autonomous space of objective intellectual constructs, of thoughts-in-themselves, equivalent to Popper's (1978) third "world" of reality (Lakatos, 1971). For Majone (1981, p. 25):

> A policy, like a theory, is a cluster of conclusions in search of a premise; not the least important task of analysis is discovering the premises that make a set of conclusions internally consistent, and convincing to the widest possible audience.

Understanding how the institutional arrangements of governance are conceptualised is important as it determines the way in which the state, among other actors, intervenes in tourism and related policy arenas and therefore selects instruments that are used to achieve policy goals. The focus of most discussions on policy instruments in tourism and hospitality is on their utilisation or their effects rather than on the understandings of governance that led to such instruments being selected from the range of potential options that state actors have to intervene. This is therefore a major weakness in many existing studies of tourism organisations as well as the role of the state with respect to both explaining the actions of actors and connecting to wider debates in social science theory. Operational studies are of significance, but they do not then relate back to the conceptualisations of governance and meta-governance that underlie intervention and policy choice, i.e. why should the state intervene in one way and not another? (Hall, 2014). Also, just as significantly, why do organisations – collectivities intermediate between institutions and individuals that are shaped by institutions – and their stakeholders do what they do? Given that organisational actions, behaviours, and strategies also imply theories.

Institutions

Institutions encourage and induce particular behaviours. North (1990, p. 3) suggests that institutions as the "rules of the game" or "humanly-devised structures … provide incentives and constraints to economic actors". While this is undoubtedly true, the institutional approach applies to all actors in a society although it is used in the social sciences with respect to organisational, social, and political actors, whose roles may also have economic dimensions at times. Nevertheless, while institutions are often regarded as long-lived, they are not unchanging, and can be transformed by politics to, for example, become more just, while laws and regulations and the overall rules of the game can be transformed to encourage organisations and society to move in particular directions, for example, with respect to recognition of human rights, environmental responsibilities, and the allocation of environmental costs. However,

> Not only may political institutions, political authorities, and political culture play a critical role in the definition, mobilization, and organization of interests, but the structure of political opportunities will shape the strategies of organized interests and their beliefs regarding the efficacy of different types of political action.
>
> (Immergut, 1998, p. 21)

One issue that arises is how contemporary so-called new institutional approaches differ from other approaches that seek to explain the rules and procedures that affect societies and economies? March and Olsen (1984) who coined the term in the context of political science, used it to describe the emergence of a range of different approaches that sought to explain the role of political institutions. In broader social scientific terms, this issue brings us to a core issue that lies at the heart of social, political, and economic thought, that of the relationship between agency and structure. Structure can be understood as the patterned socio-economic arrangements which influence, constrain, and enable the choices and opportunities available to individuals. Agency is the independent capability, capacity, or ability of individuals to enact and make their own choices. Different political philosophies and schools of thought give different emphasis to agency and structure, which then flows through into different understandings of governance, decision-making, and the ways within which society operates. Many commentators on new institutionalism, such as Scott (2014), position institutional theory as a middle path between utilitarian and structuralist approaches to explaining society.

Building on the work of Immergut (1998, 2006) and Scott (2014), Table 1.2 seeks to illustrate how new institutional approaches can be contrasted with other schools of social and economic thought in terms of interests, political processes, and normative notions of democracy. Importantly these should be regarded as ideal types and not as fixed categories because different understandings of institutions occur all along the continuum between the two extremes of emphasis on the centrality of structure and agency in approaches to society. All of the approaches are concerned with how the preferences of human actors', including organisations, are affected by the institutional contexts in which preferences are expressed. With the focus being "the effects of rules and procedures for aggregating individual wishes into collective decisions – whether these rules and procedures are those of formal political institutions, voluntary associations, firms, or even

Table 1.2 Institutional approach contrasted with other schools of thought

Emphasis on	Agency ◄- - - - - - - - - - - - - - - - - - ► Structure		
	Behaviouralist/Utilitarian	*Institutional*	*Structuralist/neo-Marxist/Marxist*
Interests	Preferences revealed through behaviour; each individual best judges of his or her interests	Diverse individual and collective interests; institutions influence their articulation and expression in politics	Social group and class-based interests. Also recognition of the role of elite/ruling class self-interest
Political process	Utility aggregation with efficient transmission of preferences (in politics, in the market, in interest group market)	Problem of aggregation; the form of the process affects quality and results of participation	Correspond to social/class structure and struggle. Objective social interests often stymied by ruling class/elite
Normative notion of democracy	Formal democracy: fairness of process guarantees justness of results: formally open access to markets/politics; competition protected	Procedural democracy: substantive justice through formal procedure	Substantive democracy: Social harmony–organic solidarity

Source: After Immergut, 1998; Scott, 2014.

cognitive or interpretive frameworks" (Immergut, 1998, p. 25). Although Immergut (1998, 2006) suggests that there is a common agenda there are certainly different approaches within new institutionalism which, in great part, reflect the relative importance attached to agency and structure, including the persistence of structure over time, as well as whether authors are coming out of economics, sociology, political sciences, planning, or organisation studies. Table 1.3 details the similarities and differences between the widely categorised three types of "new" institutionalism: rational choice institutionalism, organisation theory, and historical institutionalism (Hall & Taylor, 1996; Rothstein, 1998; Peters, 2001; Immergut, 2006).

Nevertheless, Immergut (1998, 2006) suggests that given that the common research interest is the so-called "black box" between demands and ultimate outcomes (Easton, 1965), "it does not make sense to predefine the contents of this box. A standard definition of 'institution' is thus not desirable; the common research agenda is the study of institutional effects wherever, or however, they occur" (Immergut, 1998, p. 25). Indeed, she later argues that new institutionalism is nothing more than an interest in the inefficiencies of politics and the distorting effects of the political process in understanding how similarly-situated interest groups and stakeholders responded to their situations in different ways, with their claims on the state being met by different governmental responses. Yet, even if institutional theory *is* nothing more than this, and the role of formal and informal regulations, it is still important.

Conclusions and overview

This chapter has sought to provide a very brief introduction to the emergence of new institutionalism and institutional theory in a general context. In doing so it highlights that the issue of institutions is an important one within the social sciences, and for tourism and hospitality organisations, as it seeks to explain their responses to the external environment and future directions and change. Nevertheless, the re-emergence of interest in institutions in the 1980s and 1990s is marked by a variety of different approaches and emphases, although they are united in a common interest in the study of institutional effects.

This book is divided into four chapters. Chapter 1 discusses why institutional theory is an important theoretical tool to examine tourism-related phenomena. Chapter 2 provides an overview of institutional theory from various disciplines, including sociology, economics, political science, and business studies. These disciplines have their own underpinning assumptions about the formation and development of institutions. However, there is an interdisciplinary synthesis around the links between networks between

Table 1.3 Types of new institutionalisms: similarities and differences

	Rational choice/Positive political theory	Organisation theory/Sociological institutionalism	Historical institutionalism
Interests	Strategic factors cause rational actors to choose suboptimal equilibria (e.g. tragedy of the commons)	Actors do not necessarily know the full range of their interests, limits of time, and information cause them to rely on sequencing and other processing rules (bounded rationality)	Actors' interpretations of their interests shaped by collective organisations and institutions that show traces of their own history
Political process	Without rules for ordering, cannot arrive at public interest; rules and regulations for voting, partitioning into jurisdictions, for example, affects outcomes (Buchanan & Tullock, 1962; Riker, 1980, 1982; Elster, 1986)	Inter- and intra-organisational processes shape outcomes, efforts to achieve administrative reorganisation, and policy implementation	Political process structured by constitutions and political institutions, state structures, state-interest group relations, policy networks, contingencies of timing
Normative	Understands behaviour based on micro-economic models of individual choice (Buchanan & Tullock, 1962; Riker, 1980, 1982; Elster, 1986)	norms of "appropriateness" and "standard operating procedures" as guides to behaviour (Perrow, 1986; DiMaggio & Powell, 1991; Powell & DiMaggio, 1991)	The past influences the present day through a variety of mechanisms. Historical studies tend to combine elements of rationalistic and constructivist explanation (Lowi, 1979). Interest in path-dependency (Pierson, 2000)
Actors	Rational	Cognitively bounded	Self-reflective (social, cultural, and historical norms, but reinvention of tradition)
Power	Ability to act unilaterally	Depends on the position in the organisational hierarchy	Depends on recognition by the state, access to decision-making, political representation, and mental constructs
Institutional mechanisms	Structuring of options through rules (reliance on norms controversial)	Structuring of options and calculations of interest through procedures, routines, scripts, frames (implies norms)	Structuring of options, calculation of interests, and formation of goals by rules, structures, norms, and ideas

Source: After Immergut, 1998, 2006.

different actors and the development of the institutional environment. Chapter 3 discusses the analysis of institutional logics, institutional effectiveness and enforcement, legitimation, and governance. The chapter then discusses the issue of organisational survival and change over time through the lens of the relative "mortality" of organisations. Chapter 4 examines the utility of different research methods for "doing" institutional theory and outlines some potential future research directions. The concluding chapter also returns the reader to some of the issues surrounding the structure/ agency debate and the role of institutional theory as a means to try and reconcile these major forces on organisational and individual behaviour. It also reflects on the impact of institutions on the undertaking of research. Examples and cases from tourism and hospitality are used throughout.

Issues of organisations, regulations, and change are fundamental to the understanding of tourism and hospitality and its research. Although no single theory can necessarily do justice to the rich, multi-layered levels of cause and effect that influence the organisational life of tourism and hospitality firms and destination organisations, this book contends that institutional theory can help provide rich explanations and insights into organisational behaviour and change. Given the enormous challenges faced by tourism and hospitality organisations in light of COVID-19 and the climate and environmental crisis, and an increasingly complex regulatory and consumer environment, an improved understanding of the institutional environment may assist organisations to not only survive, but thrive in meeting stakeholder demands.

2 Disciplinary foundations

Institutional theory in the social sciences

Introduction

This chapter provides a broad introduction to the disciplinary foundations of institutional theory in the social sciences and its relevance to tourism studies. It is divided into five main sections. The first four are primarily disciplinary based and discuss institutional theory from the literature in sociology, political science, economics, and international business and management. The relevance for tourism and examples from the tourism literature are noted throughout. The final section concludes that the chapter provides an integrative perspective on institutional theory within the different disciplinary fields.

Institutional theory in sociology

From an institutional perspective, sociology examines the links between institution–organisation interactions (e.g. Meyer, 2008; Scott, 2005), institutional and organisation change (e.g. D'Aunno et al., 2000), and organisational responses to institutional complexity (e.g. Ahmadjian, 2016; Greenwood et al., 2011). One of the key institutional theory perspectives that arises from sociology is the fact that institutional development is driven by individuals, organisations, and national systems (Meyer, 2008). The national system consists of institutions that evolve because of the institutional environment's historical development (Ahmadjian, 2016). The process of institutional development prescribes how different actors, including organisations and governments, behave (Meyer, 2008).

From a sociological perspective, one of the most popular theoretical lenses used to examine the institutional environment is based on the three institutional pillars: regulative, normative, and cultural–cognitive (Scott, 1995, 2001, 2008). The three pillars provide a foundation for analysing institutional environments (Palthe, 2014), and they are often used to study organisational behaviours and institutional effects on society (e.g. Child & Tsai, 2005; Hoffman, 1999). In a tourism context, for example, Suharko et al. (2018) use the three pillars approach to study the halal tourism industry. They argue that halal tourism

> can be understood as an institution, in which a set of norms and rules are to be conformed [to] by various organisations within it. Generally, wide-ranging organisations considered in the study of tourism include the government, public authorities, travel agencies, hotels, restaurants, and other interest groups, such as mass media and local communities.
> (Suharko et al., 2018, p. 337; see also Box 2.4)

The three pillars should work together to create a stable institutional environment (Scott, 2005). Scott's (1995) framework of the three pillars is an important platform from which to investigate the institutional environment and how it shapes organisational operations, because it enables the examination of organisational behaviour and operations.

Regulative pillar

The regulative pillar consists of formal rules, laws, and regulations; the logic behind it is that individuals create rules and regulations that best represent their own interests. The regulative pillar helps evaluate regulatory processes and their capability for establishing and managing rules and laws. The regulative system is viewed as a formal environment (Palthe, 2014), and organisations are obliged to obey the rules and laws within this scene (Meyer & Scott, 1983; Scott, 1995). The government often adjusts rules and regulations to make the regulative environment more stable (Alexander, 2012). This has been done, for example, in response to the COVID-19 pandemic by many of the world's governments and often specifically directed at the travel and tourism industries, given that they were among some of the most affected sectors (Loi et al., 2020; see Box 2.1). Organisations can be resilient to these changes because it is time-consuming to integrate them into the internal organisational structure (Palthe, 2014). If an organisation does not comply with the changes, the government can impose punishments in the form of sanctions (Scott, 2008). The regulative pillar includes sanctioning activities, such as rewards and punishments, to explain the behaviours of different actors (Scott, 2008). Depending on organisational responses to regulative changes, organisational behaviours and sanction outcomes can vary.

Although the regulative pillar is popular among rational choice scholars (e.g. Coase, 1937; North, 1990; Williamson, 1991), social scientists emphasise that rule-making and human behaviour are driven by individuals' emotions (Scott, 1995, 2008; Selznick, 1957; Suchman, 1995). To understand how the regulative pillar operates, it is important to study its interaction with the other two pillars, as regulations do not exist in isolation, and their development is socially embedded (Scott, 1995; Palthe, 2014).

BOX 2.1 THE REACTIONS OF GOVERNMENT AND GAMING CONCESSIONAIRES TO COVID-19 IN MACAO

COVID-19 posed a major challenge to the tourism industry and governments throughout the world. Loi et al. (2020) examined the government's measures with respect to COVID-19 and their impact on the hospitality industry in Macao, the world's most densely populated city and a major international gaming and hospitality destination. They found that the effective and successful use of regulative institutions by the Macao government stimulated autonomous actions that led to the development of new ideas and innovations, beyond compliance practice and boosted CSR among Macao's major integrated resorts. As they observed,

> All those autonomous actions taken by the gaming concessionaires (operators of the integrated resorts in Macao) may not be easily comprehensible and possible in their current scale and speed (from the outside world) if Macau government does not regulate the industry.

With the authors concluding "The Macao government has executed successfully the institutionalisation process where conception such as norms, values, social roles, behaviour, or beliefs are embedded in society and organisations. This institutionalisation process has adjusted the institutional logic of individuals and organisations".

Normative pillar

The normative pillar includes professional societal bodies that outline rules and expectations for certain groups, including organisations (Scott, 1995). It covers values and norms.

Values are conceptions of the preferred or the desirable together with the construction of standards to which existing structures or behaviours can be compared and assessed. Norms specify how things should be done; they define legitimate means to pursue valued ends.

(Scott, 2008, p. 64)

These values and norms are benchmarks for how actors are supposed to behave. Values and norms change because actor expectations may differ and are situation- and context-specific. These changes can present external pressures for organisations as they must conform or decouple from them (Oliver, 1991).

Cultural–cognitive pillar

The cultural–cognitive pillar refers to accepted beliefs shared among individuals through social interactions that guide behaviour. DiMaggio and Powell (1983) and Scott (1995) contend that this pillar constitutes the nature of social reality, and is instrumental to creating institutional meaning. Meaning is the subjective interpretation of an object, emerging as a result of interactions between actors, and is driven by cultural elements. Behavioural patterns and actions are guided to some extent by cognitive frameworks where culture plays a substantial role. The cultural–cognitive pillar examines cultural frameworks that shape internal interpretive processes (Scott, 1995). This is applicable to the formation of internal business activities and their interpretation by different actors.

Table 2.1 depicts some of the key perspectives of sociology. Selznick (1957) coined the concept of institutionalisation, defining it as a process of organisational adaptation to the challenges of the external environment. He treated institutionalisation as a process of instilling values into organisations, and as something that changes over time. Berger and Luckmann (1967, p. 54) contributed to Selznick's (1957) definition of institutionalisation by noting that, "institutionalization occurs whenever there is a reciprocal typification of habitualised action by types of actors". This implies that actors such as governments and organisations can create institutionalised rules, leading to their habitual behaviour (Berger & Luckmann, 1967). However, the problem with organisations' habitual behaviour is that institutions such as rules and regulations evolve, meaning that habitual behaviours and practices can stagnate as formal institutions change (Suchman, 1995).

Meyer and Rowan (1977) suggest that institutionalised rules or shared beliefs are incorporated into society (Table 2.1). Institutionalised rules are defined as "classifications built into society as reciprocated typifications or interpretations" (Berger & Luckmann, 1967, p. 54). Although some

Table 2.1 Institutional theory in sociology – key perspectives and their descriptions

Key concepts	Description	Studies
Institutionalisation	Adaptation to external challenges A process of instilling values into organisations Habitual behaviour of various actors	Selznick (1957)Berger & Luckmann (1967)
Institutionalised rules	Conformity to organisational rules leads to achieving legitimacy Decoupling	Meyer & Rowan (1977)
Institutional pressures and strategic responses	Five strategic responses: acquiescence, compromise, avoidance, defiance, manipulation	Oliver (1991)
Managing legitimacy	Larger institutional ecology presents challenges to managing legitimacy	Suchman (1995)
Incorporating new and old institutionalism	Develop provocations to traditional institutional principles	Kostova et al. (2008)

institutionalised rules can also be deeply embedded into organisational structures, their interpretations can be subject to the differing beliefs and values of external actors, such as governments and administrative authorities (Ahlstrom et al., 2008). External support from the actors involved can be maximised if organisations comply with existing rules, treating institutionalised rules as myths. However, complying with the rules can be ceremonial when organisations engage in decoupling. This can lead to an increasing gap between an organisation's formal structures and business activities (Meyer & Rowan, 1977).

To deal with the institutional pressures that formal structures may present, organisations employ strategic responses, including acquiescence, compromise, avoidance, defiance, and manipulation (Oliver, 1991). Acquiescence occurs when organisations accept institutional pressures by taking existing rules for granted, imitating already established strategies, or complying with the rules. Compromise is found through balancing or pacifying institutional pressures, and by engaging in negotiations with the actors involved. Organisations can also avoid institutional pressures by concealing the fact that they do not conform to the rules, or by detaching the organisation from the institutional environment, which may lead to escaping the unstable environment. When organisational goals and interests differ completely from those of other actors, including the government, organisations tend to employ a defiance strategy. In this situation, organisations can ignore or challenge the rules by opposing the existing institutional pressures. If, by engaging in defiance, organisations are unable to overcome institutional pressures, they turn to manipulating other organisations' influence and changing the formation of regulations. Manipulation is defined as "the purposeful and opportunistic attempt to co-opt, influence or control institutional pressures and evaluations" (Oliver, 1991, p. 157), and is considered the most active strategic response, because it can help organisations shift the norms and beliefs of the appropriate actors by opportunistically forming relations with them (Oliver, 1991).

Institutional pressures arise from the external environment, the formation of which is influenced by the government (Boddewyn, 2016; Wang et al., 2013). When organisations choose which strategic response to take, their decision is usually influenced by the government because of its rule-making authoritative power (Delios, 2010). Given that organisations exist as part of a larger institutional ecology, they must deal with economic, political, and socio-cultural changes (Suchman, 1995), which makes responding to institutional pressures even more complex (Greenwood et al., 2011).

Multi-national enterprises (MNEs), such as international airlines, hotel chains, and tour operators, operate in multiple institutional environments, making it extremely challenging for them to manage their operations (Kostova et al., 2008). MNEs must handle different actors, including governments, in several countries, which can be difficult because of the various actors' different interests. National, regional, and local governments form a country's regulatory system, which MNEs must navigate (Wang et al., 2013). Consequently, they need to build and manage relationships with home and host governments to facilitate their international activities (Boddewyn, 2016; Kostova et al., 2008). In addition, there is a further set of supranational and international regulatory and governance structures that have been put in place as a result of multilateral and bilateral international agreements, which also impact the institutional environments of firms and NGOs.

Institutional theory enhances understanding of the more complex aspects of social structure (Scott, 2005), where formal and informal institutions are used to enable organisations to operate within such multi-faceted environments (North, 1990). Informal institutions are widely deployed in business activities, and are often perceived as having a positive effect on MNEs' operations (Dau, 2016; Peng et al., 2008).

The development of a country's business environment is largely related to the changes that occur in the institutional environment (DiMaggio & Powell, 1983; Oliver, 1991; Scott, 2005; Suchman, 1995), what Roth and Kostova (2003) refer to as "institutional baggage". Since MNEs must navigate various institutional environments, this intensifies the complexity of institutional processes (Greenwood et al., 2011; Roth & Kostova, 2003). For example, many emerging economies (EEs), especially in Eastern Europe, have experienced dramatic institutional changes since the early 1990s (Puffer et al., 2016). MNEs from EEs have therefore had to learn to operate in unstable institutional environments, although this may be an advantage when expanding into foreign markets with similar environments (Luo et al., 2017). However, it can also be a disadvantage, because MNEs from EEs can be seen as lacking legitimacy in developed markets, which may affect their reputation and internationalisation process.

Institutional theory in political science

Institutions have been referred to as "the roots of political science" (Peters, 2012, p. 1). Old institutionalism was based on two theoretical foundations: behaviouralism and rational choice. Both imply that individuals make their decisions autonomously, regardless of formal and informal institutional intervention. However, formal rules and regulations are necessary to control human behaviour and are integral to institutional governance and the wider effects of institutions on societies (Peters, 2012). March and Olsen (1984) argue that new institutionalism emphasises the relative autonomy of political institutions, the possibilities for inefficiency in history, and the importance of symbolic action to an understanding of politics. Nevertheless, Immergut (1998) observes that suggestions of a new institutionalism are met with substantial scepticism by some scholars given that institutions "have been a focus of political science since its inception ... and, hence, plans to 'bring it back in' do not seem especially innovative" (Immergut, 1998, p. 5).

> Further confusion has arisen because the new institutionalists do not propose one generally accepted definition of an institution, nor do they appear to share a common research program or methodology. In fact, three separate branches of scholarship – rational choice, organization theory, and historical institutionalism – all lay claim to the label, seemingly without adhering to an overarching theoretical framework.
>
> (Immergut, 1998, p. 5)

Nevertheless, the different varieties of new institutionalists are all "concerned with the difficulties of ascertaining what human actors want when the preferences expressed in politics are so radically affected by the institutional contexts in which these preferences are voiced" (Immergut, 1998, p. 25) and they therefore provide valuable insights into the development of institutions and the state. Table 2.2 summarises some of the key perspectives in the shift from old to new institutionalism in political science.

One key perspective of old and new institutionalism is *legalism*. Pioneering studies (e.g. Damaska, 1986; Wilson, 1898) are solely concerned with formal institutions, laws, and regulations and their influence on the governance process of creating a state (Peters, 2012). The law serves as a foundation for analysing political knowledge. However, new institutionalists argue that this school of thought only provides the starting point for future analyses, because the law is a human creation and an evolutionary process (Evans et al., 1985). People make their choices based on

Table 2.2 A summary of old and new institutionalism in political science

Key perspectives	Old institutionalism	New institutionalism
Legalism	Focus on laws and their central role in governing	People create laws and contribute to their development
Structuralism	Structure determines behaviour	Formalisation ignores crucial informal facets
	Focus on what major institutional features are in political systems	Focus on how these characteristics function
	No link between the state and society	Advocates for collective action
Holism	Comparative analysis of the whole system	Comparative analysis of individual institutions within systems
	Countries are considered *sui generis*	Bringing in political realities of different settings
	Separation of the political environment from its cultural and socio-economic roots	The political environment derives from cultural and socio-economic roots.
	Does not allow for generalisation	Generalisation is important
Historical	Politics influenced by history	Contradictory views:
	Politics and society can influence each other	1) History is necessary to understand the contemporary political environment;
		2) Individuals' calculated behaviour predicts their actions
		Society influences political life
Normative analysis	Values and norms are seen as one unit of analysis	Values and norms are seen as separate units of analysis

Source: After Peters 2001, 2012.

institutional availability that emerges over time. Thus, while formal institutions are important, their use is not limited to formal settings, as they surround people and various actors contribute to their development.

Another perspective is *structuralism*. Old institutionalism contends that political structure shapes the behaviour of various actors, and that individuals within the government have no effect on its structure (Wilson, 1898). In old institutionalism, the focus is on the description of major institutional features that are usually used in formal settings (Peters, 2012). By contrast, the new school of thought critiques this, suggesting that such an extreme type of formalisation ignores important informal institutions and makes the study of political science too ethnocentric (Macridis, 1968). Instead of focusing simply on features of the political environment, their functionality and stability become the focus for examining institutional environments (Levitsky & Murillo, 2009; Peters, 2012). However, without knowing what the features of a political environment are, it is problematic to examine their functionality and stability. To gain a complete understanding of institutional development, identifying the features and their functionality within the institutional environment is equally important.

Holism is another perspective used to understand the development of institutions. Old institutionalism studies are predominantly comparative in nature, and compare aspects of the legal system to attain the whole picture. Conversely, new institutionalism focuses on individual legislation or constituents of institutions and how they fit into the entire political system. The pioneering studies are descriptive as opposed to comparative, as the countries are considered *sui generis*. This does not leave much room for generalisation, which new institutionalists argue is vital if the intention is to comprehend the entire political system (Dogan & Pelassy, 1990). Although countries may have distinctive features, they may also share common elements that can help create more efficient political mechanisms.

Another critical aspect of old institutionalism is its reliance on rational choice, thus divorcing political roots from their cultural and socio-economic environment, which new institutionalists challenge (Kitschelt, 2000; Peters, 2012). The link between political and social institutions is evident, and enables the study of how organisations make choices (Kitschelt, 2000). This link also allows for greater exploration of the interactions between formal and informal institutions.

A *historical* perspective has been important to the development of institutional theory in political science (Peters, 2012), with history being fundamental to studying the development of formal institutions, such as the state and its functions. Similarly, institutional theory has a pronounced historical foundation – political systems are influenced by history, and this is arguably the most shared view between old and new institutionalists. However, rational choice assumptions are also influential in new institutionalism, suggesting that individuals' calculated behaviour is the dominant predictor of their actions, as opposed to the foundations of history. Moreover, new institutionalism views the interaction between political and socio-economic environments as moving from society to politics. The old view is that this interaction can go both ways (Peters, 2012).

Normative analysis is the final perspective illustrated in Table 2.2. Old institutionalism suggests that political science emerged from normative roots, and facts and social norms were seen as a single unit of analysis that helped investigate the government and its progress based on factual data (Dewey, 1938). New institutionalism challenges this assumption by proposing that facts and norms should be viewed as separate units of analysis to better understand the functions of the government. Both views have biases, although new institutionalism uses different and more complex language to obscure them. While the normative aspect is important, new institutionalism advocates for collective action and the importance of institutions and organisations in unfolding the puzzling notion of political life. Thus, there is a need for flexibility in the analyses and methodologies of political science (Peters, 2012).

Old and new institutionalism both offer valuable insights for examining institutional environments within and between states. While old institutionalism focuses on concrete laws and regulations that determine a state's institutional infrastructure, new institutionalism introduces the importance of people in examining institutional environments. Because governments comprise a group of people who govern the state, their part in creating and enforcing formal institutions is crucial; informal institutions are created and enforced as a result of different actors' political and social interactions.

In political science, legitimacy is viewed as a "moralization of political authority" (Crook, 1987, p. 553), which means that the existing rules have a moral connotation, and compliance with these rules is based on the public perception of what is right and wrong (Beetham, 1993). The public builds its perception on the ability of the political system and the government to engrain into society the belief that existing institutions are appropriate (Lipset, 1959). The government's ability to persuade the public is driven by the effectiveness of policy development and performance (McDonough et al., 1986). The judgement of policy development and performance is based on whether the government acts in the public's best interest. The challenge the government faces is to ensure that policies target a wider range of groups with different perceptions and legitimacy judgements. This is important for the government and the state to gain and maintain political legitimacy.

The focus in political science is on legitimacy at the macro level, particularly the political legitimacy of the state and government (Allee &

Huth, 2006; Crook, 1987; McDonough et al., 1986). The state's political legitimacy is built on the historical development of the governance system (McDonough et al., 1986). For example, the changes in the governance system in Africa from colonial administration to parliamentary government in 1951 divided the perception of the legitimacy of that country. The groups that pushed for preserving existing laws and regulations challenged the legitimacy of the new legal system, while other groups of society supported the more liberal approach. As a result, Africa's legitimacy grew stronger, because the groups that favoured a more liberal approach expected that the new policies would offer the public economic and societal benefits (Crook, 1987). Changes to a political system can thus affect a state's political stability by enhancing or weakening its legitimacy (Gilley, 2006). Politically unstable states are more likely to experience weakening legitimacy because of negative public perception (Gilley, 2006). The government can influence society's perception by manipulating the necessary policies and institutions to create a more positive image of their implementation (Barnett, 1990; Mulaj, 2011).

The state's legitimacy can also change, and consequently affect governmental legitimacy (McDonough et al., 1986). Government legitimacy is judged by the effectiveness of policy development and enforcement and its outcomes for society (O'Kane, 1993). Beetham (1991) states that the quality of subordinates' performances determines a government's effectiveness. The government can achieve the same outcomes for society by engaging in military actions and/or sanctions, which can also affect its effectiveness (O'Kane, 1993). Simply obeying government requirements because it is considered a more powerful actor within a state's political system does not strengthen government legitimacy (Gilley, 2006). When enforcing policies, the government must decide which actors those policies should most affect (Beetham, 1991). Some actors may view the government as legitimate because they favour a policy that works to their advantage, but if the political system negatively affects the state's economic development, those actors can, in turn, view the state negatively (Gilley, 2006; O'Kane, 1993).

Political science scholars often view the government as holding legitimation power over decision-making and policymaking (Beetham, 1991; Crook, 1987). This is true to a degree, although to achieve legitimacy, the government has to establish relationships with the public, because the public evaluates and judges the government's actions (McDonough et al., 1986). This evaluation and judgement are often driven by the information available to the public, although information availability can also be tailored by the media to suit the desired outcome. Furthermore, the relationship between the public and the government can be influenced by the development of the state, which significantly affects public perception (McDonough et al., 1986). For example, during the Soviet era, Stalin and Lenin were strong leaders whom many Russian people respected and idolised. They served as legitimacy symbols for Russia and built its political legitimacy by creating a personal legitimacy in which people believed for decades (Gilison, 1967). This illustrates that the government has the power to not only establish the state's political legitimacy, but to ensure that its ideology is carried through history.

Legitimacy in political science literature is often associated with power and authority (Beetham, 1993; Crook, 1987; Smith, 1951; Mulaj, 2011). Smith (1951, p. 693) explains power as "the capacity to effect results". The government is seen as a powerful actor with the capacity and authority to influence results by developing and manipulating appropriate policies, which helps shape public perception (McDonough et al., 1986). Power should be exercised according to existing rules, and political authority can enhance the government's political power if used rightfully (Beetham, 1991). However, if the government engages in illegitimate behaviour, breaching the rules, the consequences can destroy the political system's order in a state through crisis or riots (Beetham, 1991). O'Kane (1993) argues that the political power of the government alone is not enough to examine legitimacy. A government's experience and past performance can contribute to explaining its behaviour, and this includes its capacity to build and sustain appropriate institutions (Evans, 1995).

The state's political legitimacy can be sustained by the appropriate institutions, despite changes in the government. In theory, the government holds legitimating power by making sure that the institutions it creates are adequate for public wellbeing (O'Kane, 1993). In practice, institutions can also influence the government's legitimation power (Mulaj, 2011). Traditionally, political scientists considered institutions to be very formal structural entities (Macridis, 1968). This assumption was applicable to Western countries because of differences with, or lack of constitutional structures in, less developed countries. The development of post-communist formal institutions in countries, such as China and Russia, illustrates the weight informal institutions had on the transformation of formal institutions (Grzymala-Busse, 2010). Although the government creates formal institutions, it does not hold the absolute power to sustain appropriate institutions because of the emergence of different actors, including organisations and non-government organisations that challenge existing institutional beliefs (Macdonald, 2008; Peters, 2012). This is important, because political science examines the government's wider role in the development of the institutional environment, but also acknowledges the involvement of other actors in this process (Macdonald, 2008; O'Kane, 1993).

Institutional interplay is defined as a collection of norms that shape patterns of behaviour (Fadda, 2012). Fadda (2012) distinguishes between formal and informal rules, contending that both have similarly functioning structures. Informal rules are not codified, but they may have formal structures – for example, religion or the church. Helmke and Levitsky (2004) note that scholars often treat informal institutions and informal organisations as the same, although the authors distinguish between the two, defining the former as shared beliefs and the latter as including clans and illegal organisations, such as the mafia. Shared beliefs emerge as a result of the state's institutional development (Cudworth et al., 2007; Köllner, 2013). This does not imply that informal organisations and institutions collide (Grzymala-Busse, 2010; Peters, 2012). By contrast, informal institutions can be readily incorporated into informal organisations (Grzymala-Busse, 2010). This is evident when personal networks are used in mafia circles, enabling them to run their operations (Helmke & Levitsky, 2004). Informal institutions can also be incorporated into formal organisations (Evans et al., 1985). For example, organisations use personal relationships to overcome the bureaucracy of the institutional environment (Tsai, 2016). Formal and informal institutions are intertwined, and their interaction is a large part of organisations' everyday behaviour.

Helmke and Levitsky (2004) provide a typology of informal institutions consisting of complementary, substitutive, accommodating, and competing categories. The first dimension of the typology is the effectiveness of formal institutions, which is measured by the extent to which written rules and procedures are enforced and obeyed in practice. The second dimension of the typology is the level of the outcome at which formal and informal institutions converge or diverge. That is, if actors follow informal rules, will the expected outcome be similar or different compared with if they obey formal rules? Since informal rules are unwritten (North, 1990), it is challenging to assess whether they have been followed. Formal rules are created by the government, and are easier to measure because they are written (Lauth, 2004). However, organisations can also influence policy creation (Lawton et al., 2013). Both institutions are an integral part of institutional environments, and their interplay is influenced by the effectiveness of their use by different actors, including governments and organisations (Lawton et al., 2013; Scholz & Wei, 1986).

For the interplay between formal and informal institutions to be complementary, both types of institution have to be effective (Figure 2.1). Fadda (2012) states that formal and informal rules can coincide; that is, there is no conflict that arises between them, and they co-evolve simultaneously. When the institutional environment is stable, institutions develop simultaneously and co-exist (Fadda, 2012; Helmke & Levitsky, 2004). Formal and informal institutions complement one another's existence and functions. This implies that the mechanisms the government uses to create and enforce regulations

Formal norms prevail over informal, in the sense that the patterns originally based on different informal rules are either modified by formal rules or are considered illegal and repressed	**Formal and informal rules perfectly coincide**
Informal norms parallel formal ones, filling spaces that are empty and actually shaping patterns of behaviour that are not regulated by formal sources, as it is often the case in developing countries.	**Informal norms prevail over formal ones**, in the sense that patterns of behaviour are actually shaped by informal norms, and either these are bound to influence and modify the formal ones or simply they coexist, with the latter being ineffective. The enforcement of formal norms can, in these cases, be either too costly or impossible.

Figure 2.1 The interplay of formal and informal institutions. Source: After Fadda, 2012.

are well established and effective. As a result, regulations have a positive effect on MNEs' development. Moreover, the relationship between the government and actors who are part of institutional environments is deployed to achieve a common goal and make the institutional environment more stable (Helmke & Levitsky, 2004; Köllner, 2013). Therefore, informal institutions can also be effective.

The accommodating type of interplay occurs when formal institutions are effective and informal institutions are ineffective. As with complementary interplay, the government plays an important role in creating and enforcing the rules and regulations. Informal institutions are usually established by actors who do not like the outcomes of formal rules and cannot openly change those rules (Helmke & Levitsky, 2004). These actors use personal and business connections to overcome stable formal institutions to achieve their goals; this suggests that they ignore existing rules and advance their interests by manipulating existing formal institutions. Although regulations exist and many MNEs follow them, they do not necessarily help MNEs reach their targets, which are often set by the home government or other key stakeholders. Informal institutions can be inefficient but can accommodate formal institutions and enable actors to reach their goals.

In the scenario where formal institutions prevail over informal, the latter can be modified (Fadda, 2012; Tsai, 2006). The stability of the institutional environment can influence the effectiveness of formal institutions by being more structured (Helmke & Levitsky, 2004). The prevalence of formal institutions is often associated with developed countries, such as the US, where the legal system is strong. Consequently, if different actors use informal institutions ineffectively, they can be modified to accommodate the formal institutions (Azari & Smith, 2012; Tsai, 2016).

Another type of institutional interplay is substitutive, which implies that formal institutions are ineffective and informal ones are effective. When this type of interplay occurs, informal institutions prevail over formal ones (Fadda, 2012). Rules and regulations exist, but their enforcement is lacking, usually because the government does not have efficient mechanisms in place to achieve this (Helmke & Levitsky, 2004; Lauth, 2004). Therefore, different actors, including MNEs, employ informal institutions to substitute these missing formal mechanisms so they can achieve their goals (Grzymala-Busse, 2010). Governments also use informal institutions, particularly established relationships, to overcome poorly executed mechanisms (Evans, 1995), and they can deploy informal institutions to enhance the formal institutional environment.

When the institutional interplay is substitutive, informal institutions can be adaptive if they are used creatively to reform existing formal institutions (Tsai, 2006). If formal institutions remain ineffective following this reformation, political actors may turn to illegal actions to pursue their agenda (Tsai, 2016). This can directly affect existing formal institutions by undermining and/or replacing them (Grzymala-Busse, 2010). As a result, in such cases, the institutional environment can become unstable over time (Tsai, 2016).

Another type of interplay presented in the typology is conflicting: where formal and informal institutions are ineffective. Both types of institution exist, but key actors do not enforce and implement them systematically because there are no mechanisms in place (Helmke & Levitsky, 2004). These actors might follow one rule, but to do so, they break another (Helmke & Levitsky, 2004). The use of informal institutions is also ineffective because the interests of different actors, such as government and MNEs, conflict, which negatively affects their relationships. This also negatively influences the development of the institutional environment as a whole. Therefore, the relationship between formal and informal institutions is conflicting.

The four types of institutional interplay present a key aspect of the institutional environment (Fadda, 2012). Each type of interplay illustrates that governments and organisations enable the development of the institutional environment. In fact, the way organisations use informal institutions can illustrate the flaws in existing regulations, because informal institutions are often used to fulfil incompetent and formal regulations (Tsai, 2006). Understanding the way each type of institutional interplay influences the dynamics of the institutional environment can facilitate an examination of its nuances.

Institutional theory in economics

Institutional theory in economics originated in the late 19th century in
Germany and Austria and was further shaped by US scholars. Veblen (1909)
challenged the traditional assumption that individual behaviour is calculated
and contended that individual behaviour is driven by habits (see Table 2.3).
Veblen (1919) further suggested that individual behaviour changed as the
institutional surroundings evolved. Therefore, individual behaviour within
organisations carries an institutional character. Veblen (1919) focused on
the effect of individuals and groups on institutional development, but did
not explain the role of institutions in organisational activities. Individuals
and groups, including the government, are crucial to the development of
institutions that influence the behaviour and operations of organisations.

Commons (1924) added to Veblen's (1909, 1919) view by arguing that
individual choice in behaviour is driven by transactions, a process between
two or more parties in an environment where mechanisms and rules of

Table 2.3 Institutional theory in economics – key perspectives and their descriptions

Key perspectives	Description	Exemplary studies
Individual behaviour is related to the institutional character	Individual behaviour is governed by the institutional character Institutional character changes because of changes in institutional environments	Veblen (1909, 1919)
Individual choice behaviour is governed by transaction	The transaction is seen as a process between two or more parties where rules of conduct and formal mechanisms prevail Rules of conduct are social institutions Focus on broader social and political factors that affect the economic structure	Commons (1924)
Transaction cost economics	Exchange within a firm is governed by rules and hierarchy and not a price mechanism Transaction costs include the cost of negotiating and a contract for each exchange transaction	Coase (1937)
Transaction cost economics	The effectiveness of transaction cost depends on two conditions: bounded rationality and individual opportunism	Williamson (1975, 1985, 1991)
Notion of game	Formal and informal institutions. Focus on macro analysis	North (1990, 1991); North & Weingast (1989)

conduct dominate. He referred to rules of conduct as social institutions, or institutional rules that provide boundaries for individuals and companies so they can achieve their goals. This implies that social institutions and rules are socially embedded. Coase (1937) posited that the transaction process is based on exchange within an organisation, which is governed by hierarchically enforced rules. Therefore, the transaction process is seen as the exchange that incurs the cost of negotiating a business transaction (Williamson, 1975). The boundaries outlined by the established rules enable organisations to rationally engage in the opportunism provided during this exchange process (Williamson, 1985, 1991). This school of thought facilitates examining how organisations operate within various governance structures.

The governance structure within a national state comprises cultural, political, and legal environments, within which formal and informal institutions create the 'rules of the game' (North, 1990). North (1990, 1991) refers to formal institutions as constitutions, laws, property rights, and sanctions, and to informal institutions as taboos, values, customs, and traditions. Institutional economists view institutions as being dominated by a regulatory system, where rules and their enforcement mechanisms play a dominant role when examining the institutional environment (North & Weingast, 1989). The state develops the rules and enforcement mechanisms (North, 1990). However, the state sometimes acts with its own interests as the primary concern and serves as rule maker, referee, and enforcer during the exchange process between different actors (Evans et al., 1985).

The exchange process unfolds as a result of networking, which underscores the importance of informal institutions in developing the institutional environment (North, 1991; Williamson, 1985). Although the state makes and enforces rules and regulations, various actors' interpretations of these rules and regulations may differ. North (1991) states that societies have been using these forms of institutions for thousands of years in trade exchanges, such as those within and beyond local trade. This is important, because the relationships that have emerged between different actors are not simply an exchange process. Rather, they have been driven by the creation of formal and informal institutions and are based on political and economic ties between parties. The fact that both formal and informal institutions can be used by the actors involved illustrates that these institutions do not develop in a vacuum, and that their use is strategic.

Institutional theory in business studies

Marketing

Since the call for addressing institutional analysis more rigorously was made by Yang and Su (2014), the examination of institutional theory in business marketing has grown significantly (Theingi et al., 2017). Institutional theory has been applied to marketing in several ways. The application of Scott's (1987) framework of the three pillars of institutions has been a popular theoretical tool to examine the role of the institutional environment in marketing channels (Grewal & Dharwadkar, 2002). Theingi et al. (2017) found that several institutional constraints, such as poor communication channels and lack of rural and regional infrastructure, influence the use of formal and informal marketing channels. Formal marketing channels should help to build stronger networks with domestic institutions such as banks. However, these formal channels present intense competition for informal channel members (Theingi et al., 2017). The two different channel structures can seriously jeopardise the legitimacy of regulative, normative, and cognitive pillars. As a result, the institutional environment becomes more complex for host organisations to operate.

Several studies applied the three institutional pillars perspective to examine differences between business networks in various markets (Jansson et al., 2007). Jansson et al. (2007) found that business networks in China, Russia, and Western Europe play a different role and are managed in different ways because of the contextual differences in the institutional environments in these markets. Furthermore, the overlap between personal and business networks influence the changes in institutional environments as well as network structures (Mattsson & Salmi, 2013). Accounting for contextual factors is crucial when studying institutional environments and networks and marketing discipline allows to examine the link between the two concepts.

Institutionalism has also been a focus in marketing with regards to the associations between different actors. Arndt (1981, p. 37) defined institutions as "sets of conditions and rules for transactions and other interactions" and where culture is often considered as an informal structure of a wider social setting. Arndt (1981) argues that institutionalisation can provide an exciting platform for the interplay between markets, politics, and hierarchies. Their interplay in fact contributes to the development of the idiosyncratic features of the institutional environment, which in fact influences marketing practices and enhances entrepreneurial processes that are embedded in this environment (Webb et al., 2011). These studies illustrate the importance of examining the link between different constructs. However, when applying institutional theory to relationship networks, it is crucial to account for situational factors (Yang & Su, 2014) because relationships, networks, and institutional environments are not static (Morrish & Earl, 2020).

International business and management – dealing with institutional complexity

Institutional complexity has been documented in numerous international business and management studies (Meyer & Höllerer, 2016; Meyer &

Rowan, 1977; Raaijmakers et al., 2015; Ramus et al., 2016; Raynard, 2016) and has been referred to as a 'third wave' of institutional theory (Johansen & Waldorff, 2015). Institutional complexity arises when organisations face "incompatible perspectives from multiple institutional logics" (Greenwood et al., 2011, p. 318). The international business literature focuses on conflicting institutional logics, primarily in relation to inter-institutional complexity, where institutional logics are examined in different institutional environments (Greenwood et al., 2011). Understanding conflicting institutional logics is important for studying institutional complexity as an aggregate (Saka-Helmhout et al., 2016). However, these conflicting elements, especially between different levels of governments, can be a strategic advantage in MNEs' internationalisation process (Luo et al., 2017). MNEs can use their relationship with government officials to gain resources and access networks, which enhances their operations. Further, conflicting institutions can act as learning mechanisms that MNEs can employ to manage institutional complexity (Desai, 2016; Marano & Kostova, 2016; Ramus et al., 2016). Therefore, there is a need to examine the nuances of institutional complexity.

When institutional complexity has been examined previously, the focus has been on field structure and organisational attributes, including position in the field, ownership (Greenwood et al., 2011), and knowledge about institutional infrastructure (Dau, 2016). The nature of institutional complexity is significantly influenced by the structure of the field in which organisations operate. The structure within the field is driven by institutional logics that shape the behaviours of relevant actors (Scott, 2008). Because actors use logics flexibly to enhance outcomes, the structure of the field becomes less transparent, thus increasing institutional complexity (McPherson & Sauder, 2013). An example of such behaviour is evident in EEs, where flexible logics are used purposefully as tools to influence court decisions in favour of MNEs or governments (McPherson & Sauder, 2013). For example, Russia's federal government uses logics flexibly to form formal institutions, which allows them to adapt and interpret laws and regulations in their favour (Black & Tarassova, 2003). In China, Chen et al. (2016) argue that there are multiple logics associated with tourism development, including the logic of pursuing political legitimacy (discussed further below), the logic of fiscal income maximisation, the dual logics of the market and politics, and the logic of pursuing economic benefits. Significantly, with respect to the complexity of the environment within which businesses operate, they note that these logics also operate at multiple scales: national, regional, and local.

This flexibility of applying institutional logics to interpreting formal rules fragments the structure of the field, thus increasing institutional complexity

(Greenwood et al., 2011; McPherson & Sauder, 2013). In less fragmented markets, the regulations are more unified, which should decrease institutional complexity (Meyer, et al., 1987). While this does apply in some industries, such as education (Meyer et al., 1987), fragmentation can lead to increased institutional complexity in other industries because of conflicting institutional logics (Greenwood et al., 2011). In the case of tourism in Macau, for example, Fong et al. (2018) suggest that tourism actors responded to changes in institutional factors by adopting an institutional logic of coopetition, which included five key processes: exploiting, exploring, bridging, sharing, and boundary spanning, as part of the co-evolution between the multi-stakeholders' changing logics of practice and the surrounding institutional environment.

MNEs being positioned in a strategic sector can be an organisational attribute, whereby MNEs use their position in the field to deal with institutional complexity (Marano & Kostova, 2016). This is possible when organisations engage in learning and become catalysts for identifying strategies for managing institutional complexity, especially where the institutional environment is weak (Desai, 2016; Marano & Kostova, 2016). Organisations that are not in strategic sectors are less likely to obey established institutional practices because they are not bound by institutionalised relationships with different actors. Conversely, organisations operating in strategic sectors are often the centre of media, government, and society attention. This means that many MNEs are more likely to follow institutionalised practices (Ahmadjian & Robinson, 2001). MNEs may follow the existing practices on the surface, but in reality, how they handle institutional complexity can be less visible because of their desire to protect their actor-specific relationships (Kostova et al., 2008).

Studies have focused on the organisational response to institutional complexity based on competing or incompatible institutions (Bertels & Lawrence, 2016; Faulconbridge & Muzio, 2016; Saka-Helmhout et al., 2016). The responses are influenced by institutions and their enforcement mechanisms that exist in a particular market. Ahmadjian (2016, p. 13) proposes that "national systems, the specific institutions that define and distinguish these systems, and the mechanisms by which institutions combine into distinctive configurations, they share a fundamental assertion that national institutional systems shape the strategy, structure, and fundamental assumptions of firms". How MNEs create these configurations is influenced by existing institutions and their enforcement mechanisms, which are developed by the government (Peters, 2012). Therefore, before examining MNEs' responses to intra-institutional complexity, we must understand what institutional complexity actually comprises.

Managing intra-institutional complexity is a crucial step in the internationalisation process, yet it has been largely neglected in the international business literature (Meyer & Höllerer, 2014, 2016) and is clearly also crucial for international tourism businesses. Intra-institutional complexity is a vital part of MNEs' development and internationalisation because they must first navigate the domestic institutional environment (Kraatz & Block, 2008; Meyer & Höllerer, 2016). Meyer and Höllerer (2016, p. 2) refer to intra-institutional complexity as "conflicting institutional demands that arise within the same institutional order". One area where this has been particularly important in a tourism context is with respect to the development of public–private partnerships, which are often marked by considerable tensions between the different logics of the public and private good (Saz-Carranza & Longo, 2012). This clearly implies that institutional logics can be in conflict with one another (Thornton, 2002). Intra-institutional complexity is therefore strongly influenced by the institutional environment of a particular context.

Legitimacy

Legitimacy has gained substantial attention in institutional theory, particularly in relation to MNEs and how they gain and manage legitimacy (Bitektine & Haack, 2015; Deephouse et al., 2017; Kostova & Zaheer, 1999; Suchman, 1995; Suddaby et al., 2017). However, it is a topic that is surprisingly little discussed in a tourism setting. With the work of Ruhanen and Whitford (2018) on racism as an inhibitor to the organisational legitimacy of indigenous tourism businesses in Australia and Zapata and Hall (2012) on balancing legitimacy and effectiveness in local public–private tourism partnerships in Spain being notable exceptions.

Table 2.4 summarises some of the key studies that define and/or describe legitimacy in a business and organisational context. The importance of legitimacy has been recognised as a key element in social life, and in political and governance regimes (Weber, 1947). Originally, legitimacy was analysed at the macro level, by examining its influence on social life. Weber (1947) further extended this and examined legitimacy in relation to a process of change in values and beliefs and organisational reliance on rational or legal structures. Organisations are considered legitimate if they conform to these structures. However, social functions must be considered when determining organisational behaviour, because organisations sometimes base their actions on broader social beliefs (Parsons, 1960).

Maurer (1971, p. 361) ascribed hierarchical connotations to legitimacy, contending that "legitimation is the process whereby an organisation justifies to a peer or superordinate system its right to exist". Based on this

Table 2.4 Legitimacy – definitions and descriptions

Sources	Definitions/descriptions	Emphasis
Weber (1947)	A process of change in values and beliefs and organisational reliance on rational or legal structures	The emphasis is on the legal system, where organisations make a rational choice to conform to rules.
Maurer (1971)	Legitimation: the process whereby an organisation justifies its right to exist to a peer or superordinate system	Organisations have the right to justify their legitimate existence in a hierarchical system.
Dowling & Pfeffer (1975)	Congruence between the social values associated with or implied by activities and the norms of acceptable behaviour in the larger social system	Organisational legitimacy is driven by their involvement in social and political activities.
Meyer & Scott (1983)	The degree of cultural support for an organisation – the extent to which the array of established cultural accounts provides explanations for an organisation's existence and functioning	Cultural aspects affect the existence and functioning of organisations. Cultural aspects influence organisational legitimacy.
Suchman (1995)	A generalised perception or assumption that an entity's actions are desirable, proper or appropriate within some socially constructed system of norms, values, and beliefs	Organisational legitimacy is influenced by the stability of an institutional environment.
Deephouse (1996)	Social actors' endorsement of an organisation	Organisations do not have to satisfy all the actors. The most important actors are government regulators and public opinion. Establishing legitimacy in foreign markets depends on the size, age, performance and reputation of an MNE as a whole.
Kostova & Zaheer (1999)	An organisation's acceptance by its environment	Cultural adaptations and the nature of the product and regulatory environment also affect legitimacy.

(Continued)

Table 2.4 Continued

Sources	Definitions/descriptions	Emphasis
Zimmerman & Zeitz (2002)	A relationship between the practices and utterances of the organisation and those that are contained within, approved of and enforced by the social system in which the organisation exists	A social judgement of acceptance, appropriateness and/or desirability.
Kostova et al. (2008)	It is impossible to achieve legitimacy through isomorphism because of the multiplicity and complexity of the institutional environment	An alternative mechanism that multi-national corporations employ in negotiating their status with relevant actors.
Bitektine & Haack (2015)	The degree of an organisation's collective approval	Organisational legitimacy consists of two components: individual-level propriety and collective-level validity. Legitimacy process under conditions of institutional stability and change is affected differently.

definition, organisations have the right to justify their operations to the superior actor and be judged by this actor. Dowling and Pfeffer (1975) further developed Parsons' (1960) idea of conformity to social beliefs, referring to it as cultural conformity, but not to the hierarchical system or self-justification. They viewed legitimacy as accepted behaviour in a larger social system (Dowling & Pfeffer, 1975). This acceptance is determined by similar values between an organisation and political and social systems. These values are culturally embedded – therefore, the acceptance of organisational behaviour is influenced by cultural aspects in a particular context (Meyer & Scott, 1983). Cultural factors can explain organisational legitimacy and the extent of its existence and functioning, as culture is part of the larger social environment in which organisations operate (Meyer & Scott, 1983). The legitimation process for organisations becomes complex because they must comply with cultural and regulatory norms that influence different actors' perceptions of their actions (Bitektine, 2011; Xu & Shenkar, 2002). In the case of Ruhanen and Whitford's (2018) research on Aboriginal tourism businesses in Australia, such a perspective was critical because the culturally dominant norms of racism and discrimination in Australian society were seen to directly impact the extent to which indigenous businesses were perceived and regarded as "legitimate" businesses.

Suchman (1995, p. 574) states that organisational legitimacy is "a generalized perception or assumption that the actions of an entity are desirable, proper, or appropriate within some socially constructed system of norms, values and beliefs". Whether the actions are perceived as desirable, proper, or appropriate depends on the actors who judge the organisation's behaviour. These actors form certain norms and rules that organisations follow to act properly. However, organisations need only satisfy actors whose perceptions will affect their operations (Elsbach & Sutton, 1992). Deephouse (1996) states that the government and public are the most important actors, because the government develops the regulatory framework and the public influences the social norms that form the environment in which organisations operate. The challenge organisations face is that they cannot satisfy the interests of all actors – therefore, the legitimation process becomes more complex, as organisations must prioritise whose acceptance is more desirable (Deephouse, 1996).

An organisation's acceptance by its environment is an important part of organisational legitimacy (Kostova & Zaheer, 1999). The environment consists of cultural norms and regulations, which affect whether the organisation is accepted within it. From this perspective, organisational legitimacy is socially constructed and dependent on the collective beliefs of specific social groups, including the government and the public (Bitektine & Haack, 2015; Scott, 1995; Suchman, 1995). Therefore, legitimacy can be described as a relationship between the practices and regulations of approved organisations and enforced by a larger social environment in which organisations operate (Zimmerman & Zeitz, 2002). An organisation's practices and regulations both influence organisational legitimacy and its enforcement. Such an observation is extremely important in the case of tourism businesses, CSR policies, behaviours, and actions, for example, which have become an increasingly important element of demands for more sustainable forms of tourism (Aureli et al., 2017; Remondino et al., 2019; see Box 2.2). Although, arguably, from a tourism perspective, issues of legitimacy can also be extended from specific businesses to also include the broader destination context with respect to branding; for example, in terms of how green or sustainable a destination may be. Therefore, there is also potential to use an institutional lens to investigate the legitimacy of destination brand narratives as well as of the destination management/marketing organisations and other public agencies that support them (Samkin & Schneider, 2010).

BOX 2.2 CORPORATE SOCIAL RESPONSIBILITY (CSR) AND SUSTAINABILITY INITIATIVES OF MULTI-NATIONAL HOTEL CORPORATIONS

Ng and Tavitiyaman (2020) undertook a study of the disclosures by multi-national hotel corporations on CSR and sustainability matters. They found that Western hotel corporations had an emphasis on integrated innovation management (IIMs) and utilised global measurement approaches and standards such as GRI standard and ISO14001 certification. In contrast, and potentially reflecting different institutional environments, Asian hotel corporations were found to have diverse CSR and sustainability initiatives in terms of public relation management (PRMs) (e.g. staff development, staff remuneration and welfare, and good stewards of the environment) and enterprise risk management (ERMs) (e.g. operational risks management, use of solar energy, and new energy conservation) approaches, but a low implementation of IIMs.

The existing regulations and actual practices that organisations undertake to gain legitimacy are related (Tost, 2011). Organisations may view legitimacy purely as a resource owned by that organisation, independent of the perceptions of different actors (Zimmerman & Zeitz, 2002). Organisations may not obey regulations if they interfere with achieving the main organisational objectives and may instead engage in illegitimate activities to acquire legitimacy (Elsbach & Sutton, 1992; Suchman, 1995). In an environment where regulations diverge from practice, organisations engage in negotiations with relevant stakeholders to attain legitimacy (Kostova et al., 2008) because existing institutions are not suited to meet the objectives of these organisations (Thornton et al., 2012). However, it is important to recognise that it is the government that has the power to set and enforce the rules and regulations (Boddewyn, 2016). Therefore, organisations must negotiate with the government, which implies that legitimacy can also be enforced via regulatory actions or other governmental measures, such as threats of action. This means that organisations and governments can both influence the enforcement of organisational legitimacy (Cuervo-Cazurra et al., 2014), with the relationships between the two influencing how various actors perceive and enforce legitimacy.

Negotiation and enforcement imply that an organisation's legitimacy is approved collectively (Bitektine & Haack, 2015). Different actors, including the government, determine the approval and evaluation of legitimacy (Díez-Martín et al., 2013; Scott, 1995). However, organisations can use legitimacy as a resource to gain access to other resources, such as networks, financial and human capital, and technology (Zimmerman & Zeitz, 2002). Although legitimacy can be viewed as a resource, individuals approve an organisation's practices as appropriate, and then collective actors, including the government and organisation, make a collective judgement or reach a consensus about the organisation's legitimacy (Bitektine & Haack, 2015). The notion of collective judgement becomes interesting in the case of an MNE, because the collective judgement occurs in home and host countries (Cuervo-Cazurra et al., 2014). For example, perceptions of animal and even human rights may be different in source countries and at destinations creating significant issues for outbound tour companies to manage as although behaviours may be acceptable at the destination, governmental and public pressures to change activities provided to tourists (Font et al., 2019; Yang, 2020; Zapata Campos et al., 2018). While the process of judgement and approval can be driven by home and host governments (Rottig, 2016), MNEs can engage in silenced legitimation of judgement, where the government and MNEs may conceal the undesirable legitimacy outcome from the public (Bitektine & Haack, 2015). In this case, organisational legitimacy can be generalised (Tost, 2011). MNEs can therefore use their relationships with the government to orchestrate perceptions of their actions, and hence establish and maintain legitimacy in various markets.

Types of legitimacy

Another stream of business studies literature focuses on different types of legitimacy, which are summarised in Table 2.5. The traditional view is that organisational legitimacy is driven primarily by external factors (Suchman, 1995; Weber, 1947). This view underscores the importance of political regimes to which organisations must conform. An equally crucial view is the importance of external and internal factors that determine organisational legitimacy (Drori & Honig, 2013). This view recognises the influence of external actors and internal organisational attributes on legitimising organisations.

Suchman (1995) identified three types of legitimacy, pragmatic, moral, and cognitive. Pragmatic legitimacy relates to the self-interest of an organisation and relevant actors, which is based on a direct exchange between them. There are three different types of pragmatic legitimacy: exchange, influence, and dispositional (Suchman, 1995). Exchange legitimacy is based on an exchange between actors who are driven by their own interests and

Table 2.5 Types of legitimacy and their descriptions

Type of legitimacy	Description	Source
Pragmatic: • exchange legitimacy • influence legitimacy • dispositional legitimacy	Rests of the self-interested calculations of an organisation's most immediate actors. Rational choice.	Suchman (1995, p. 578)
Normative (moral) • consequential • procedural • structural • personal	Reflects a positive, normative evaluation of the organisation and its activities.	Suchman (1995, p. 579)
Cognitive	Organisational objectives and activities are based on the values that the society sees as appropriate, proper, and desirable.	Suchman (1995, p. 579)
External Internal	Acceptance and validation by external stakeholders. The acceptance or normative validation of an organisational strategy through the consensus of its participants, which acts as a tool that reinforces organisational practices and mobilises organisational members around a common ethical, strategic or ideological vision.	Drori & Honig (2013, p. 347) Drori & Honig (2013, p. 347)

can scrutinise the organisation during this exchange (Dowling & Pfeffer, 1975; Elsbach & Sutton, 1992). Influence legitimacy is when actors support the organisation because of their interests. Dispositional legitimacy is when organisations and actors share the same values and interests and are trustworthy (Scott, 1995). All three types of pragmatic legitimacy are based on the relevant actors' judgement of the organisation. Although the judgement is based on self-interest, it is also somewhat socially driven (Bitektine, 2011). Tost (2011) argues that because the legitimacy judgement is influenced by different actors, the perception of organisational legitimacy can be generalised.

Normative or moral legitimacy is based on whether the organisational activities are the right thing to do (Suchman, 1995). Relevant actors define what is right or wrong by judging and approving or disapproving an organisation's behaviour. There are four types of moral legitimacy: consequential, procedural, structural, and personal (Suchman, 1995). Consequential legitimacy is a judgement of what organisations have achieved, and is based on performance and measurement of these organisational achievements. These measurements reflect an organisation's effectiveness and the extent of its contribution to social welfare (Scott, 2008). Procedural legitimacy is achieved if organisations embrace socially accepted procedures. Structural legitimacy is similar to procedural legitimacy, although it focuses on the entire organisational system, whereas procedural legitimacy focuses on organisational routines (Scott, 2008). Personal legitimacy is based on "the charisma of individual organisational leaders" (Suchman, 1995, p. 581) and their ability to communicate with different actors (Patel et al., 2005). Different actors can judge charisma in various ways – it is thus challenging to judge legitimacy based on individual characteristics. The judgement is often determined by an organisation's contribution to the market's social welfare (Tost, 2011) or to broader notions of public and environmental welfare.

Cognitive legitimacy is considered to be the most powerful type of legitimacy because it is "based on cognition rather than on interest or evaluation" (Suchman, 1995, p. 582). Cognitive legitimacy is associated with existing cultural and institutional aspects (Suchman, 1995). The pre-existence of institutions helps to determine and examine an organisation's characteristics and behaviour (Bitektine, 2011; Scott, 1995). Cultural aspects are used to examine the extent to which actors' established beliefs affect organisational legitimacy (Suchman, 1995). Based on these beliefs, the actors see the organisation's actions as legitimate or illegitimate (Suchman, 1995). They evaluate cognitive legitimacy based on the historic development of existing beliefs and regulations (Aldrich & Fiol, 1994). Cognitive legitimacy is characterised by organisational characteristics and existing rules that determine organisational legitimacy (Tost, 2011).

The three types of organisational legitimacy are linked and develop in a broader societal system (Suchman, 1995; Tost, 2011). The accountability for some degree of structure and embeddedness in the broader social system in which organisations operate is crucial to examining organisational legitimacy (Tost, 2011). External actors develop the policies and regulations within the social system, meaning that they largely influence all three types of organisational legitimacy (Kostova & Zaheer, 1999). As a result, organisations aim to balance their internal characteristics and external forces (Bitektine, 2011; Suddaby & Greenwood, 2005).

Drori and Honig (2013, p. 347) define internal legitimacy as "the acceptance or normative validation of an organisational strategy through the consensus of its participants, which acts as a tool that reinforces organisational practices and mobilizes organisational members around a common ethical, strategic or ideological vision". Internal legitimacy is important for achieving organisational objectives by obeying the codes of conduct established within the organisation (Kostova & Zaheer, 1999). Common codes stipulate certain patterns of behaviour for employees and the wider organisation (Deephouse, 1996). Internal legitimacy can be developed via employee training (Esteban-Lloret et al., 2018), and can be extremely significant with areas such as governance (Walters & Tacon, 2018), employment strategies and commitment to local populations (Forstenlechner & Mellahi, 2011), and sustainability (Loconto & Fouilleux, 2014). Internal legitimacy is therefore crucial to organisational survival and operations (Kostova & Roth, 2002), and especially for social tourism enterprises (Vestrum et al., 2017; Yang et al., 2018) given their specific commitment to the public good, although external actors can also clearly influence an organisation's reputation within the environment in which the organisation operates (Bitektine & Haack, 2015). Therefore, organisations also feel institutional pressure to satisfy external actors (Zimmerman & Zeitz, 2002). In their study of community-based music festivals that aim to improve the identity and economy of rural communities, for example, Vestrum et al. (2017) identified three legitimation strategies used by the community enterprises: conformance to the internal (rural community) environment; conformance to the external (cultural festival) environment; and changing the internal (rural community) environment.

External legitimacy is the acceptance and validation of external stakeholders, including governments and social groups (Deephouse, 1996; Drori & Honig, 2013; Rottig, 2016). Achieving external legitimacy is more challenging than achieving internal legitimacy because organisations have to satisfy a number of external actors, which can be a time-consuming process (Kostova & Zaheer, 1999). External legitimacy is also vital for organisational survival and success because external actors can influence how the organisation is perceived (Drori & Honig, 2013). Deephouse (1996) has found that the two key actors, the government and the public (whose opinion is often shaped by the media), can confer external legitimacy. The expectations of the environment in which organisations operate often differ from an organisation's internal practices (Drori & Honig, 2013). As a result, organisations engage in the institutionalisation of organisational legitimacy by adjusting their practices (Bitektine & Haack, 2015; Zapata Campos et al., 2018). This could make striking a balance between internal and external legitimacy challenging (Kostova et al., 2008; Xu & Shenkar, 2002). Organisations must continuously adjust their practices to meet the interests of external actors, which can be difficult, because the nature of the institutional environment is usually constantly changing, especially for organisations and businesses operating in an international environment. Therefore, the legitimacy type also changes (Suchman, 1995). The type of legitimacy organisations aim to achieve depends on their objectives and positioning within the market. As a result, organisational legitimacy and how it is used can be influenced by various factors.

Factors influencing organisational legitimacy

Kostova and Zaheer (1999, p. 66) identify a number of factors that influence businesses, and MNCs in particular: "the characteristics of institutional environment; the organisation's characteristics and actions; and the legitimation process by which the environment builds its perceptions of the organisation". An institutional environment's characteristics are represented by complexity and multiplicity, with tourism recognised as usually providing a more complex institutional environment than many other industries and business sectors because of the nature of the tourism system, its service dimensions, and the mobility of its consumers (Roxas & Chadee, 2013). Kostova and Zaheer (1999) propose that because the cognitive and normative pillars of an institutional environment are tacit and not easily codified, they present a challenge for MNEs to establish legitimacy in a host country. Conversely, the regulative domain is easily codified by laws and regulations, and therefore easier to follow (Scott, 1995). Established regulations serve as guidelines for businesses regarding what is right and wrong – but because the institutional environment is not static, neither are these regulations (Shipilov, 2012). This makes the institutional environment more complex and organisational legitimacy harder to achieve, because businesses must continuously adjust their operations. For example, Soares et al. (2020) noted that the institutional environment is particularly significant with respect to information and communications technology, with hotel technologies, from infrastructure to communication, being socially and technically legitimised in their institutional environment via certificates offered by platforms that legitimise hotels before users and competitors (Gretzel et al., 2017).

Changes in the institutional environment create institutional pressures that influence organisational legitimacy (Dacin et al., 2002). This is particularly relevant for businesses and MNEs from EEs and developing countries because of the institutional changes these markets have experienced since the 1990s (Rottig, 2016; Wang et al., 2018). Formal institutions are often considered unstable and filled with institutional voids, making the institutional environment more difficult to navigate (Puffer et al., 2016; Rottig, 2016). In examining the hotel sector in St Petersburg, Russia, Karhunen (2008) found that industry-level isomorphic forces were not at work during the economic transition. As a result, and combined with substantial market imperfections, significant intra-industry strategic diversity emerged. However, the underlying institutional logic shifted as the transition continued. Karhunen (2008) argued that during the transition, diversity was based on local versus foreign management and during the post-transition it was grounded more on operational legitimacy. As a result, the majority of hotels were operating according to shared norms and practices, although the lack of state coercive pressures also allowed some hotels to operate more informally and ignore institutional norms.

Kostova and Zaheer (1999) argue that unless businesses have a clear understanding of existing formal and informal rules, they will not successfully maintain legitimacy in a foreign market or in a different domestic market than the one they normally operate in (Wang et al., 2018; see Box 2.3). While understanding how formal and informal institutions work is important, knowing the nuances of the institutional voids can also affect organisational legitimacy. For example, misguided regulations formed by the government to favour a particular industry are considered a void (Khanna & Palepu, 2005; Rottig, 2016), and not knowing about these regulations can influence an organisation's ability to achieve legitimacy in that market. If a business lacks institutional knowledge, this can undermine its performance and reputation in the market (Deephouse, 1996; Rottig, 2016).

BOX 2.3 THE IMPACT OF THE INSTITUTIONAL ENVIRONMENT ON THE GEOGRAPHIC DIVERSIFICATION OF CHINESE TOURISM FIRMS

Wang et al. (2018) examined a sample of Chinese listed tourism companies with respect to the influences of local institutional environments on tourism firms' geographic diversification decisions and strategies as they sought to expand their spatial reach and grow their business and market. Their study found that institutional factors had a significant positive impact on firms' geographic diversification decisions, including with respect to the overall extent of marketisation, the relationship between local governments and the market, and the degree to which a product or market was developed. The results also show that the moderating effects of the business type indicate that tourism firms operating a non-natural or historical business have a high possibility of diversifying across regions if they are located in regions with a high degree of marketisation, a loose relationship between local governments and the market, and a developed non-public economy or a developed product market (Wang et al., 2018).

Another factor that influences organisational legitimacy is organisational characteristics, including size, performance, and reputation (Deephouse, 1996; Kostova & Zaheer, 1999). An organisation's size can affect its visibility in a market, as well as public expectations (Tost, 2011). This can shape an organisation's behaviour in that market. The relevant stakeholders' performance expectations are also important for achieving legitimacy (Kostova & Zaheer, 1999). Choosing whose expectations to meet depends on the power a stakeholder has over an organisation's legitimacy. Therefore, managing the relationship with this stakeholder is a key factor in achieving legitimacy. For example, Ahlstrom et al. (2008) suggest that to gain legitimacy in China, a company must establish a relationship with the local government because of its power to shape an organisation's reputation. A finding borne out in Wang et al.'s (2018) study of the influences of local institutional environments on Chinese tourism firms' geographic diversification strategies (see Box 2.3).

Organisational reputation can also influence legitimacy by creating a particular image of the organisation (Bitektine, 2011; Suchman, 1995; Rao, 1994) and, as noted above, is particularly significant with respect to CSR and sustainability reputation. Further, reputation can enable businesses and

MNEs to develop relationships with key stakeholders. Some scholars argue that reputation and legitimacy should be separated to gain a deeper conceptual understanding of organisational legitimacy, but the two concepts are closely interrelated (Bitektine, 2011; Rao, 1994). For example, a strong reputation can enhance strategic practices by deviating from standard practices and remaining legitimate. Reputation can also contribute to attaining different types of legitimacy – for example, when an organisation is striving to achieve normative legitimacy, a strong reputation for transparency and accountability is necessary (Deephouse & Carter, 2005). This may be extremely important, for example, with emissions reporting by tourism and transport companies, so that comments regarding positive commitments to reducing climate change impacts and promoting sustainability can be matched by clear information on carbon footprint (Scott et al., 2016; Zeppel, 2012). Both concepts allow for an examination of organisational behaviour, which is executed through the process of judgement by relevant stakeholders (Bitektine, 2011). Reputation is complementary to organisational legitimacy and judgement because it contributes to building an organisation's image in a particular market (Rao, 1994).

Another factor that can influence organisational legitimacy is the legitimation process, which is referred to as "the process through which legitimacy is achieved" (Kostova & Zaheer, 1999, p. 73). The legitimation process is influenced by the institutional environment as well as organisations. The institutional environment defines the rules and regulations that organisations must follow, which, to an extent, shapes the way organisations operate and are perceived by external actors (Bitektine & Haack, 2015). An organisation can influence the legitimation process by incorporating existing rules and regulations into internal practices (Drori & Honig, 2013). The legitimation process is complex because of its social and cognitive nature. Organisations operating in a particular legal field will need to obey the existing rules and regulations relevant to the field that organisations operate in. Depending on the development of the institutional environment, they may have to adjust any standards that do not fit with the existing internal practices (Drori & Honig, 2013). In tourism, a common way to meet standards is to undergo public, i.e. governmental, or private accreditation according to a predefined set of standards, and these may relate to such issues as health and safety (Labonté et al., 2018; Mehta et al., 2017), sustainability (Baird et al., 2018; Font et al., 2019; Gössling & Buckley, 2016; Hughes & Scheyvens, 2016), or even religious standards, such as halal or kosher (Hall & Prayag, 2020; Box 2.4). Organisations can employ various strategies to overcome legitimation issues in domestic and foreign markets.

**BOX 2.4 HALAL ACCREDITATION
AND CERTIFICATION**

"Halal" is one of the Islamic principles that refers to what is lawful and permissible for Muslims to consume and practice. It is one of the core customs and practices observed in Islam in addition to the five fundamental pillars of Islam (Arkan al-Islam): belief in the only God, Allah, and Muhammad as the last prophet (shahadah), pray five times a day (salat), pay almsgiving (zakat), practice fasting in Ramadan month (sawm), and make a pilgrimage to Mecca at least once in a lifetime during the month of pilgrimage (hajj), which is obligatory for Muslims. Consuming what is lawful and permissible is stipulated in Islamic laws (also referred to as Shariah), which frames the principles of Islam based on the Quran (the sacred book of Islam), the Hadith (collected reports describing the Prophet Muhammad (peace be upon him)), Sunnah (traditions and habitual practice in Islamic communities), and the fiqh (Islamic jurisprudence). The five commandments (al-ahkam al-khamsah): obligatory (wajib/fard), recommended (mandub), permissible (mubah), discouraged (makruh), and prohibited (haram) are a network of rules in social, spiritual, cultural and every aspects of Muslims' life.

Islam strictly dictates consuming halal and makes distinctions between halal and haram (an opposite concept to halal that indicates what is unlawful and prohibited for Muslims) in the Quran. Although there is a great deal of commonality in understanding what is halal and haram, there are different interpretations of the Quranic verses as a result of different schools and teachings; customary practices (Razak et al., 2020); and time, place, and circumstances (Armanios & Ergene, 2018; Riaz & Chaudry, 2004). Table 2.6 provides an overview of the main elements of halal and kosher foods.

With the growth of travel to and from Muslim majority countries and the internationalisation of trade, attention to the consumption and production of hospitality and tourism products by and for Muslims has become increasingly formalised and regulated with the development of a number of national halal certification and accreditation programmes, although there is no single international standard for halal. Halal certification is undertaken worldwide. Despite the fact that there are common understandings of halal, each halal certification awarding body has different standards, requirements, and processes that may be influenced by different teachings, cultures, and other factors. As a result, the absence of a universal halal standard

Table 2.6 Comparative summary of the differences between halal and kosher food

Description	Halal	Kosher
Pork, genus Sus, and carnivorous animals and their by-products	X	X
Meat slaughtering	Complying *Shariah* (Islamic law)	Complying *Kashrut* (Jewish dietary law)
Blood	X	X
Dairy	Made with halal enzymes	Made with kosher enzymes
Blessing/invocation	On each animal while slaughtering	Prior to entering the slaughtering area
Insects and by-products	Locust and its by-products accepted Others X	Grasshopper accepted By-products X
Seafood	Vary by degree of acceptance	X
Fish	Generally accepted, some with scales and fins only	With scales and fins only
Alcohol	X	O (grape-based products have strict production requirements)
Fasting	O	O
Plants	O (except intoxicants and alcohol)	O
Segregation of meat and dairy	N/A	O
Segregation in the food supply chain	Between halal and non-halal food	Between meat, dairy, and neutral products (*pareve* – contain neither dairy nor meat ingredients)
In case of doubt	Avoid	Consult Rabbi
Animal welfare	O	O
Hygiene, sanitation	Thorough cleaning Idle period not required	Cleaning Idle period required Ritual cleaning (kosherisation)

Note: In this table, "O" means permissible; "X" means not permissible.
Source: Adapted and modified from Razak et al. (2020) and Riaz and Chaudry (2004).

increases institutional complexity for consumers and food manufacturers (Latif, 2020; Latif et al., 2014).

Halal certification is an assurance of products as being halal issued by a halal certification awarding body and has been developed in response to the internationalisation of the trade in food and other products as well as consumer concerns as to product authenticity and the security of supply chains. In order to ensure the integrity, sometimes referred to as halalness, of halal products, several governments have established a set of institutional arrangements to manage halal certification and/or authenticity. Various mechanisms have been employed, including specific halal related legislation, inclusion under consumer law, and the creation of and/or recognition of halal certification bodies by the government. Halal certification systems have been developed in a number of countries and legal jurisdictions, including Malaysia, which established the first standards in 1974; Indonesia; Brunei; UAE; Qatar; Saudi Arabia; Oman; Kuwait; Bahrain; some states in the USA – California, Maryland, Michigan, Minnesota, New York, Texas; Canada; and Singapore. Obtaining halal certification can take a number of forms, including examinations and the implementation of processes by the halal certification awarding body that requires a high standard of cleanliness, high-quality products, and compliance with Islamic laws from producers, suppliers, and sellers. However, the procedures and requirements can vary greatly between different halal authorities.

Riaz and Chaudry (2004) categorised halal certification in terms of registration of a site (or a business) certification, certification for a product for a certain period of time, and yearly certification. Site registration certification is awarded to a site that is inspected and approved to manufacture, distribute, or market halal food, e.g. a plant, production facilities, abattoir, slaughterhouse, restaurant, and any establishment of handling food. However, this type of certification is confined to the boundary of the site and should not be used for a product or service available outside of that site. Product certification is issued for a specific period or quantity of the product. If for quantity, it is described as a batch or shipment certification where each batch or consignment needs to be certified. Yearly certification requires annual inspection through halal compliance and guidelines, and payment of a fee to the certification body is usually required. This type of certification may require a fixed renewal period for certification upon inspection or may be automatically renewed upon inspection or any other requirement from the certification awarding bodies.

There were more than 300 recognised halal certification awarding bodies globally in 2018 (Hall & Prayag, 2020), and each body has its distinctive logo. These bodies can be a government, Islamic community, or organisation; an NGO; a private business; or even an individual Muslim. Regenstein et al. (2014) identified resource availability, willingness to cooperate and work with the company on problem-solving, ability to explain their halal standard and fee structure in a clear manner, and acceptability among consumers and importers as significant factors in certification. In other words, awarding bodies must possess authenticity, credibility, and recognition in order to be recognised as a credible halal certification awarding body.

Each halal certification awarding body has its own standard and requirement, which may differ from others. In the Food and Agriculture Organization's (FAO) general guidelines for the use of the term "halal" (CAC/GL 24-1997), *The Codex Alimentarius*, which is globally recognised as a global food code, standard, and guideline, it states:

> The Codex Alimentarius Commission accepts that there may be minor differences in opinion in the interpretation of lawful and unlawful animals and in the slaughter act, according to the different Islamic Schools of Thought. As such, these general guidelines are subjected to the interpretation of the appropriate authorities of the importing countries. However, the certificates granted by the religious authorities of the exporting country should be accepted in principle by the importing country, except when the latter provides justification for other specific requirements.
>
> (FAO & World Health Organization [WHO], 2001, p. 1)

Different procedures and schemes are applied in different halal certifications. In general, the products first meet local guidelines on quality and safety standard, then they can be considered for halal certification. The halal certification process generally starts with the application and submission of the required documents (e.g. ingredients, facility, and hygiene), followed by an audit, and finally the issuance of halal certification (Latif, 2020; Riaz & Chaudry, 2004).

The differences between halal certification awarding bodies are significant and are not purely administrative, because of the implications for export as well as different markets (Riaz & Chaudry, 2004). If a market area or target is a specific country, then it is important to choose a certification that is widely recognised and acceptable in that country.

Muslim majority countries like Indonesia, Brunei, Malaysia, Turkey, and the Gulf Cooperation Council (henceforth GCC) countries have made huge efforts to ensure and promote halal food internationally, especially given the growth in demand and their desire to develop their food manufacturing sectors. Many governments have developed halal standards and regulations for halal food in order to assure consumers of the authenticity of their halal food products as well as create a market niche for them in the international halal marketplace.

Partly as a result of the competition between countries to be halal hubs, the recognition of foreign halal certification is substantially different between countries. The Malaysian authority (JAKIM) recognised 84 foreign halal certifications as of February 2020, while its Indonesian counterpart (MUI) recognised only 45 foreign halal certification bodies in May 2020. The appointment of foreign halal certification is supposedly made based on compliance with the guidelines of bodies such as JAKIM or MUI. Foreign halal certification bodies are required to be monitored or evaluated by MUI or submit annual reports to JAKIM to maintain their appointment. JAKIM recognises food and goods certified by the recognised foreign halal certification bodies. For example, all imported meat and its by-products to Malaysia must be halal certified by JAKIM or listed by foreign halal certification bodies. Plants are inspected by JAKIM and the Malaysian Department of Veterinary Services. The MUI categorises its recognition of foreign bodies into slaughtering, raw material, and flavour. To give an example of the implications of this, Brunei halal is only recognised by MUI under its slaughtering category; thus, only meat and by-products are recognised as halal, while processed meat-based food and goods are not recognised.

Non-Muslim majority countries, such as Australia and New Zealand, recognised the economic prospects of the halal food export market, and the governments of both countries established a regulatory halal framework in conjunction with the private sector and Islamic community associations. The Australian government issued guidelines with respect to slaughter, preparation, identification, processing, segregation, storage, and certification in order to maintain the quality of Australian manufactured or produced halal food products. New Zealand also has similar guidelines established by the government (Hall & Prayag, 2020).

Yuri Oh & C. Michael Hall

Strategies to achieve organisational legitimacy

Another stream of business literature focuses on how organisations achieve legitimacy. Many scholars state that organisations achieve legitimacy through isomorphism – that is, by adopting their practices, structures, and norms to those of the institutional environment (Aldrich & Fiol, 1994; Bitektine & Haack, 2015; Deephouse, 1996; DiMaggio & Powell, 1983; Meyer & Rowan, 1977). Meyer and Rowan (1977) introduced the notion of institutional isomorphism, where formal rules and routines within an organisation are governed by the wider institutional environment. To achieve legitimacy and gain access to the necessary resources, organisations must become isomorphic with the institutional environment in which they operate (Meyer & Scott, 1983). Therefore, organisational legitimacy can be achieved by conforming to the existing institutional environment. DiMaggio and Powell (1983) identify three mechanisms that, in practice, should induce an isomorphic change in organisations: coercive, normative, and mimetic. Isomorphism can "make organisations more similar without necessarily making them more efficient" (DiMaggio & Powell, 1983, p. 147). Coercive isomorphism arises from political influence, where businesses depend upon other actors for strategic resources. A clear example of coercive isomorphism is when a government can secure funding to attract a business to relocate or even allow it to establish a local presence and, in return, the business has to adapt its practices to support a destination's economic development (Rottig, 2016). For example, an international hotel chain may modify its guest data and online privacy practices from one destination to another in order to satisfy the requirements of host governments. Coercive isomorphism leads an organisation to conform to the regulatory environment.

Normative isomorphism can emerge from within an organisation and its authority to control how it conforms to established norms, standards, and practices (DiMaggio & Powell, 1983). Normative isomorphism is driven by professions within the organisation, which can create misalignments between internal and external legitimacy, causing the organisation to undertake illegitimate activities (Greenwood et al., 2002). Mimetic isomorphism occurs when organisations learn from and imitate the strategies of existing organisations to succeed in the market. However, imitating strategies is problematic because it does not allow for new ideas and practices to emerge (Greenwood et al., 2002). Further, because organisational attributes differ and are important to achieving organisational legitimacy (Greenwood et al., 2011), mimicking one organisation's behaviour may not be a suitable strategy.

Conformity through isomorphism restricts organisations' strategic choices, because all three types of isomorphism imply some degree of following the host market's rules (Zimmerman & Zeitz, 2002). Kostova et al. (2008) propose that there is a limited isomorphism in MNCs because of their multiplicity and ambiguity. Since MNEs operate in diverse institutional environments, the institutional pressures they face differ, and each sub-unit can, to some extent, select the strategies for adapting organisational practices and responding to institutional pressures (Kostova et al., 2008). Parent companies often impose certain obligations as to what practices can or cannot be adopted, because a sub-unit's legitimacy in a particular country can affect MNEs' legitimacy in other markets (Spencer & Gomez, 2011; Zapata Campos et al., 2018).

MNEs can use several strategies to address the challenges of achieving legitimacy. Communication strategies can enhance organisational legitimacy when information flows are managed between the company and key actors (Suchman, 1995; Suddaby & Greenwood, 2005). This allows the company to balance external and internal legitimacy, depending on which type it aims to achieve. Communication is an important element of the legitimation process because it enables businesses to manage actors' judgement (Bitektine & Haack, 2015). Businesses can achieve this by controlling the information actors receive, which can negatively or positively affect organisational legitimacy judgement (Bitektine & Haack, 2015). For example, as noted above, if a business adopts corporate social responsibility practices, this creates a positive perception of it on the part of external actors (Zheng et al., 2015; Zapata Campos et al., 2018). However, a negative effect can emerge as a result of a business' involvement in corruption or human rights abuse, which can destabilise its legitimacy and operations in some markets (Kostova & Zaheer, 1999; Muthuri & Gilbert, 2011; Pfarrer et al., 2008). In the case of encouraging tourism MNCs to combat corruption and favouritism three different strategies are available: 1) anti-corruption reform; 2) "tightrope" balancing; and 3) tolerance for corrupt practices (Windsor, 2019), with the actual strategy dependent on where perceived legitimacy is desirable. Control of information cannot be guaranteed, and how MNEs are regarded can be communicated verbally through the media or through non-verbal actions, such as selecting the right environment and manipulating external actors' perceptions (Bitektine & Haack, 2015; Suchman, 1995). This is a particularly important issue for international travel and tourism MNEs, for example, as what is acceptable in the destination with respect to things such as animal, human, and labour rights may be unacceptable in the main markets where tourists come from. In such cases, such businesses and destinations may be particularly vulnerable to negative communications (Seyfi & Hall, 2020; Zapata Campos et al., 2018).

Environment selection is another strategy that can enable organisations to achieve legitimacy (Suchman, 1995). It involves selecting the most favourable environment in which an organisation can operate as it is, without adjusting any of its practices (Zimmerman & Zeitz, 2002). In international tourism, this is possible when a tourism MNE is familiar with the rules, norms, and regulations of a host market and enters it with the right product (Suchman, 1995). However, businesses need to acquire knowledge about the logic behind developing the institutional environment of a particular market, as this can enable businesses to interpret the existing rules and regulations and make a more informed selection decision.

Manipulating the organisation's perception is another legitimation strategy, and entails changing the environment to attain consistency between the organisation's needs and the environment (Zimmerman & Zeitz, 2002). It is described as an anticipated and purposeful intervention to develop and influence specific institutions to support an organisation's operations (Dowling & Pfeffer, 1975; Oliver, 1991; Suchman, 1995). Manipulation requires a departure from existing norms, and is influenced by innovative organisations that require existing institutions to be altered (Suchman, 1995; Zimmerman & Zeitz, 2002). Organisations manipulate the environment by influencing the relevant actors' perceptions (Bitektine & Haack, 2015) – for example, by becoming part of a trade association or entering into partnerships with local investors, which can affect the manipulation of institutional logics (Suddaby & Greenwood, 2005; Pache & Santos, 2010). This strategy can also help enhance external legitimacy without adapting organisational practices (Xu & Shenkar, 2002). Manipulation is the most strategic legitimation strategy because it is purposeful (Zimmerman & Zeitz, 2002). However, the choice of strategy depends on a business's objectives.

Institutional theory: an interdisciplinary synthesis?

Although theoretical perspectives of institutional theory in the different disciplines have different emphases, there are significant intersections between them, which provides significant insights on institutional theory. Figure 2.2 illustrates four main configurations, namely, exchange

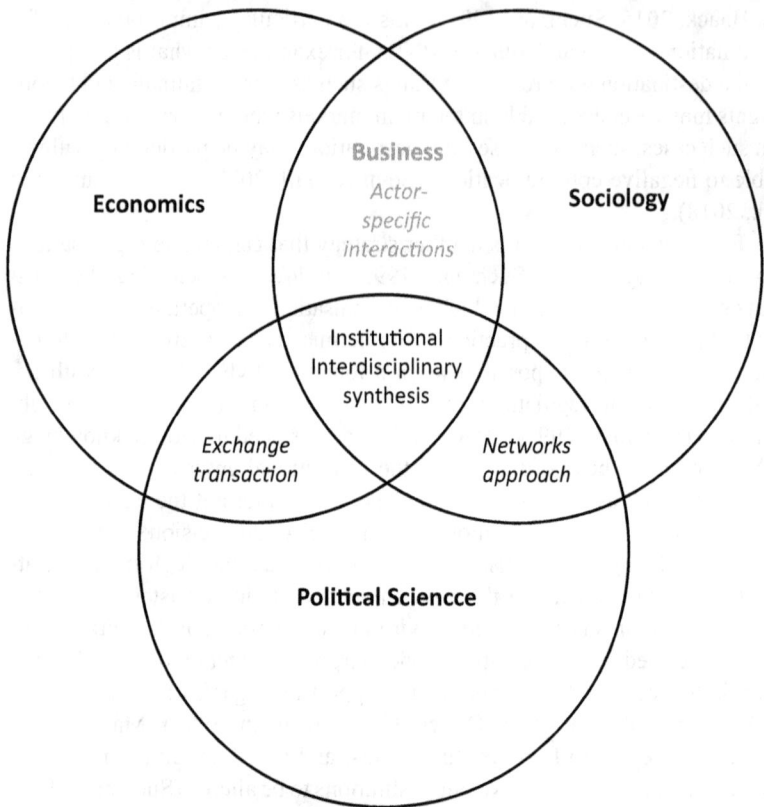

Figure 2.2 Interdisciplinary synthesis of institutional theory.

transaction, actor-specific interactions, networks approach, and institutional overlap. These various combinations provide some of the main themes of institutional theory development and application, including in a tourism context.

The first configuration is an exchange transaction that is a focus primarily in economics and political science (Figure 2.2). The transactional nature of the relationships between different actors in the national system is emphasised by both fields as well as by business studies (North, 1990; Peters, 2012). This transactional relationship is regarded as being influenced by the rational choices that involved actors make (Williamson, 1991). Political science scholars focus on political factors of the development of the state, where the government is one of the key actors, if not the major actor, facilitating the formation of formal and informal institutions (Evans, 1995; Köllner, 2013). Whereas in economics, the focus is on the transaction itself, which is driven by an exchange process between the involved parties (Coase, 1998). This exchange influences the formation of institutions, which shapes the institutional environment of the state (North, 1991) and the associated institutional arrangements, which are critical in terms of the allocation of responsibilities for policy areas, including tourism (Hall, 2008). The transactional overlap between the two disciplines illustrates the importance of formal and informal institutions in the formation of the institutional environment. Both disciplines acknowledge that institutions are socially embedded, with institutional development deriving from the formal institutional structure, which therefore gives importance to the exchange transaction between actors.

The second configuration is between sociology and political science, which is illustrated in Figure 2.2 as actor-specific interactions. The relationship between the different actors is reciprocal and has a significant impact on the formation of the institutional environment (Köllner, 2013; Meyer & Höllerer, 2014). Both sociology and political science emphasise the fact that the relationships between the actors are influenced by the existing socially embedded rules (Fadda, 2012; Meyer & Rowan, 1977). The focus in sociology is on the impact these relationships may have on organisational behaviour (Oliver, 1991; Suchman, 1995). In political science, the emphasis is placed on the structural behaviour of the formal institutional environment, such as governments, organisations, and issues of governance (Köllner, 2013; Peters, 2012). The behaviour of these actors is institutionalised, based on existing rules and values, which is a common perspective in both disciplines (Evans, 1995; Fadda, 2012; Oliver, 1991). The challenge occurs when organisations and the government have diverging interests and are faced with managing continuous changing relationships between them as a result of their diverging interests (Voronov & Weber, 2016). These relationships can be reciprocal but differ in the way they are managed.

The institutional theory in sociology and economics views networks between actors as an important component of the institutional environment, which is the third type of configuration of institutional theory which has become a major area of interest in tourism even if not necessarily viewed via the lens of institutional theory (Hall, 2008). In economics, networks are examined through the development of an institutional environment, where networks are informal institutions that traditionally enabled international trade and helped to manage relationships with foreign traders (North, 1990). Sociologists see networks as a more complex form of organisational relations that serve as mechanisms to facilitate their operations, although more formal networks can also assume an organisational life of their own. The commonality between the two disciplines is that networks are used to manage the relationships between different actors, including governments and organisations, which influences their domestic and international operations. The networks between different actors develop as a result of the relationships between them, and these networks play a crucial role in the development of the institutional environment within a state. This line of thinking is a significant development of institutional theory in business and organisational studies.

Although the institutional theory in business studies, including existing research in tourism, has been dominated by economics and sociology, political science provides great insights into the formal structure of the institutional environment of a particular state or level of governance. Indeed, research on governance in tourism has been substantially influenced by institutional theory (Hall, 2011a, 2011b; Amore & Hall, 2016). The fourth configuration is the institutional overlap of the key perspectives on institutional theory between the three disciplines (Figure 2.2), which indicates potential common ground in the development of institutional studies. However, there the various fields of study that tend to focus on different scales of analysis; for example, the focus in economics is primarily on the macro level, on how institutions impact the economic development of a country. Political science examines the institutional impact on political development and formal governance structures of a state (Evans, 1995; Peters, 2012; Tsai, 2016). Whereas sociologically influenced literature concentrates on the institutional impact of organisations' behaviour and development. All disciplines, however, acknowledge that institutions are socially embedded and treat the historical development of institutions with a high level of importance to understanding their functioning (Evans, 1995; North, 1991; Scott, 1987). Recognising that institutions are socially embedded is essential for examining how institutional environments have developed. Formal and informal institutions also co-exist, and the interplay between them makes the institutional environment more complex, but it also helps to guide organisational practices. Formal and informal institutions exist within a state, but their interplay occurs as a result of the relationships between key actors. However, critically for understanding tourism from an institutional theory perspective, this institutional interplay contributes to the institutional environment of a particular country (Fadda, 2012) and the place of tourism within it. The issues of institutional analysis and its significance for understanding tourism is discussed in further detail in the next chapter.

3 Institutional analysis

Introduction

This chapter provides a further discussion on institutional analysis and its significance for understanding tourism. It is organised into three main sections. The first discusses the multiple layers of the institutional environment. The second discusses the multi-scale institutional analysis based on competing for institutional logics, interplay, legitimisation, and governance perspectives. The chapter then considers the issue of organisational survival and change over time through the lens of the relative "mortality" of organisations. The significance of understanding tourism and examples from a range of different contexts are noted throughout the chapter.

The layers of the institutional environment

The institutional environment consists of multiple layers, because of the interaction among different actors at different levels of governance (Zhang & Merchant, 2020). The framework presented in Figure 3.1 captures these multiple layers under four headings: international, central (national), regional, and local. Businesses are positioned at the centre of this framework because they have to navigate the institutional layers every day in order to succeed. These layers are conceptualised by governments at different levels: central, regional, and local. Collaboration both within and between these layers is crucial in terms of institutional coordination, yet it can be very challenging because their functions and interests may not align.

In a case where interests diverge, the institutional environment becomes extremely complex to navigate. This is especially well recognised in federal systems, such as Australia, Canada, Germany, and the United States, where substantial divergence can occur between the state's and federal government's perspectives on certain issues. A good example of this is the responses of different US states to the COVID-19 pandemic, where different states simultaneously enacted different regulations on travel and

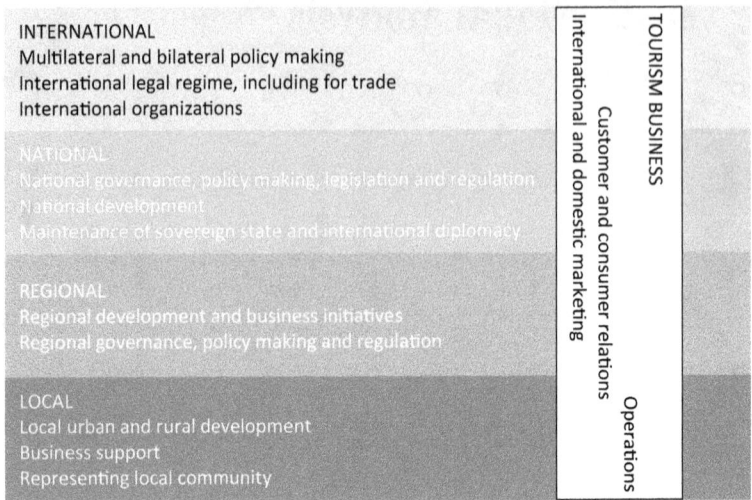

Figure 3.1 Multi-layered institutional environment for tourism businesses.

biosecurity measures in response to the disease and its economic impacts (Studdert et al., 2020; see Box 3.1). Such divergence was also mirrored in the international sphere in terms of international travel restrictions (Seyfi et al., 2020). Businesses have to understand all four layers and, just as importantly, they need to realise that they operate on all four levels. This is especially important for tourism firms because of the movement of international tourists between different institutional jurisdictions. The institutional environment is somewhat stable when the regulations are effective and the boundaries clearly defined for organisations to follow. When regulations are not effective, and there are no mechanisms in place to enforce them, organisations tend to rely on informal relationships with the governments at different levels depending on their goals; such a situation makes the institutional environment more dynamic and also increases the level of uncertainty for businesses and their strategies.

BOX 3.1 US INTERSTATE TRAVEL RESTRICTIONS DURING THE COVID-19 PANDEMIC

Travel restrictions were an integral part of the responses of national, regional, and local governments to reduce or "flatten" the curve of disease transmission. However, their use often varied substantially between jurisdictions as they sought to balance economic, health, and political considerations. By the end of September 2020, nearly half of the US states had imposed interstate travel restrictions. Eight had imposed restrictions on entrants from all states, 12 had imposed them only on entrants from selected high-prevalence areas, and four had shifted between these positions. A common feature of these restrictions was a requirement that entrants, whether residents or non-residents, had to self-quarantine for 14 days, although active monitoring of compliance to these orders appeared to vary. Several states also modified their restriction orders to permit proof of negative tests for COVID-19 infection in lieu of self-quarantining. However, in the US context, any measure that may be construed as a potential limit in interstate trade and mobility raises substantial legal issues. The US Supreme Court has long recognised an implicit constitutional right to travel, consisting of: "the right to enter and leave a state, the right 'to be treated as a welcome visitor rather than an unfriendly alien' when visiting a state, and the right to become a citizen of any state" (Studdert et al., 2020). In the US, any restrictions on the right to travel across state lines are given close legal scrutiny with respect to its appropriateness and reasonableness, although it should be noted that different courts may arrive at different conclusions. In seeking to review restriction orders and their implementation, courts are extremely mindful that there is no discrimination with respect to out-of-state visitors, for example, with respect to ease of meeting quarantine requirements. This issue is important,

> because when states treat out-of-state travellers differently, they confront greater constitutional uncertainty than when their regulations affect residents and non-residents even-handedly. Courts are mindful that, historically, differential travel restrictions have served as a pretext for turning away minorities or impoverished people and for economic protectionism. Courts also tend to be more sceptical when exceptions are granted to some interests and activities but not to other, similar ones.
>
> (Studdert et al., 2020)

As a result, health-related travel restrictions in the US travel restrictions are more likely to withstand legal scrutiny if they apply equally to residents and non-residents, allow well-justified exceptions (e.g., recent negative tests for a disease, evidence of vaccination), are time-limited and regularly reviewed, and are grounded in epidemiologic data. Nevertheless, it is notable that institutional differences and a lack of coordination were at the heart of the US national pandemic response.

> Yet state or regional isolationism is a poor substitute for national leadership in pandemic response. Even as it refused to suspend Maine's travel restrictions, the Maine court quoted Supreme Court Justice Benjamin Cardozo's admonition in *Baldwin v. Seelig*, an economic protectionism case, that "The Constitution was framed … upon the theory that the peoples of the several states must sink or swim together, and that in the long run prosperity and salvation are in union and not division". Cardozo's plea for unity could be read today as a call for the coordinated, coherent federal response to Covid-19 that has been so lacking. Such a response might have mitigated the disparities now driving interstate divisions and the desperation states feel to protect themselves when no one else will. Infectious diseases may not recognise political boundaries, but disease-control policies certainly do.
>
> (Studdert et al., 2020)

The international layer of the institutional environment is occupied by a number of international and supranational bodies that operate within specific policy areas and responsibilities. Central to these from a tourism perspective is the United Nations (UN) and its associated bodies, including the UN World Tourism Organization (UNWTO). Other significant bodies of the UN relevant to tourism include the UN Environmental Program (UNEP) and the UN Development Program (UNDP). However, arguably of even greater significance is the World Trade Organization (WTO), because of its role in setting the international structure for trade and investment, and organisations such as the OECD, for policy transfer, and the World Bank, for development funding (Carrillo-Hidalgo & Pulido-Fernández, 2019). Significantly, the emphasis on public–private partnership that is often so strong at the national and regional level is also given a strong focus internationally, for example in the UNWTO, where global tourism business interest organisations, such as the World Travel & Tourism Council (WTTC), are also important because of their influence on international and domestic policies (Coles & Hall, 2008). What is important about the international sphere is that the multilateral and bilateral agreements that are made between countries sets the context for international mobility and affects many, if not all, tourism businesses in one way or another, but so many firms are unaware or dimly aware of these critical structures and their implications for inbound, outbound, and domestic tourism.

The national layer of the institutional environment is represented by authoritative central government power over policymaking, a focus on state development, and the protection of the sovereign state. The central government has the authoritative power to make and amend policies, which are focused on developing the state (Baranov et al., 2015; Wang et al., 2020). For example, the central government usually controls treaty-making powers with other countries. For example, in Australia in the late 2020, the Morrison national government sought new legislative and regulatory powers for the foreign affairs minister to review and cancel agreements to stop state, territory and local governments, and universities from entering agreements with foreign governments that are considered by the minister to be detrimental to Australia's foreign policy (Murphy & Hurst, 2020). Although the central/national government layer of the institutional environment may seem dominating because of its authoritative ability to override decision-making in many cases, depending on the constitution of the country, networks at the regional and local levels can interfere with policy development and implementation at the national level (Kujala et al., 2020). The institutional environment is therefore not static (Shipilov., 2012), but continuously evolving. As a result, the central government's priorities can change, thus influencing the dynamics between different layers of the institutional environment.

The regional layer of the institutional environment consists of policy initiation at the regional scale, and a focus on regional development and governance. The regional government can propose policy changes or applications by the central government in relation to their region (Baranov et al., 2015). The main aim of engaging in negotiations for policy change is usually related to regional development objectives. Often, the central government has an overarching objective and sets goals for regional development targets. In cases where central, regional, and local policies aim for the same development outcomes, the institutional environment is easier to navigate.

Organisational attributes and an organisation's strategic importance in terms of developing the economy at different levels influence the institutional environment. Organisations form relationships at different layers, which places them in an interesting position, as they must manage their relationships with the government at each layer to achieve their goals. Organisations use their own resources, such as financial resources, to shape policy development. This is evident in exchange-based relations, where MNEs help fund governmental projects and in return may receive certain privileges and avoidance of administrative review. This may be particularly important in countries in which the transparency of business relations with the government is opaque. Nevertheless, in many countries, collaboration with the government at different levels help MNEs to achieve their goals as part of public–private partnerships.

The institutional environment becomes more challenging when the goals between the central, regional, and local governments diverge, as this can undermine formal institutions. This makes formal institutions more ambiguous and challenging for organisations to follow and causes them to rely more on informal institutions to achieve their goals. As a result, the importance of formal institutions decreases, whereas that of informal institutions increases. This makes the institutional environment more unstable and challenging for organisations to navigate, because the existing regulations are ambiguous (Puffer et al., 2016). Further, differing goals between organisations and governments at different layers can affect resource allocation and organisational development.

Networks between industry and government officials may be public or hidden, depending on the institutional and political context (Dang et al., 2020). In some cases, the connections between industry and government officials may be hidden because this enables organisations to better deal with a complex institutional environment. Nevertheless, in some jurisdictions, this situation shows that such silent relationships enable organisations to facilitate their operations by overcoming ambiguous regulations (Saka-Helmhout, 2020). However, such silenced relationships can have negative consequences for organisations if they are broken, and particularly if they are seen as being inappropriate. These consequences may include losing access to administrations, which presents organisations with more difficulties in terms of handling institutional complexity. For example, the grounding of the Boeing 737 Max in 2019 as a result of plane crashes revealed that there was an inappropriate closeness to the relationship between the US Federal Aviation Administration (FAA) and Boeing officials, which reduced proper scrutiny of the jet's systems and safety (Josephs, 2019). Networks with the government at all three levels serve to enable organisational interests, although the public acceptance of such networks depends on the specific political culture as to what is "normal politics" and the degree of independence from external interest that is expected of politicians and members of the bureaucracy. Nevertheless, such factors, which are often hidden in more formal accounts of political systems, affect the relative complexity of the institutional environment and the difficulties it can present for organisations, especially those derived from other political cultures and responsibilities.

In general, the relationship between corruption and tourism is only substantially discussed at an aggregate scale in the tourism literature (Poprawe,

2015; Lv & Xu, 2017; Haseeb & Azam, 2020). Interestingly, Ming and Liu (2020) examined China's anti-corruption campaign as a form of political uncertainty in China's tourism industry. They found that when the Chinese central government launched its anti-corruption campaign, firms in the tourism industry experienced a significant decline in firm value, with the effect being stronger for companies majoring in high-end tourism products. They also found that tourism companies' long-term financial performance declined after the anti-corruption campaign, with the decrease in firms' financial performance being driven by a decline in demand. However, the nature of the relationship between industry and government is one that warrants closer analysis in a tourism context. There is also something of a paradox that while governments, industries, and numerous academic commentators frequently stress the supposed importance of public–private partnerships, the development of networks and cooperative relations, there is often little discussion at what point such relationships become inappropriate. While from a governmental or public good perspective it is to be hoped that such relations will contribute to the competitiveness of tourism from a destination perspective, there must clearly become a point where individual firm benefits in such relationships become more significant for the firm than they do for the greater good. Nevertheless, such questions are clearly important as they underlie public trust in tourism-related institutions (Nunkoo et al., 2012; Roy et al., 2017).

Multi-scaled analysis

Institutional theory is a powerful tool to examine institutional environments (Paul & Feliciano-Cestero, 2020) and how they affect tourism and hospitality businesses. Because of the complexity that each layer adds to the institutional environment, it becomes more challenging to analyse it. Nevertheless, there are a number of ways in which institutional environments can be understood.

Institutional logics

Institutional complexity has been examined from the perspective of conflicting institutional logics within organisations as well as in different markets (Boone & Özcan, 2020; Greenwood et al., 2011; Saka-Helmhout et al., 2016). Institutional logics can be characterised through organising principles by which different actors "organize time and space and provide meaning to their social reality" (Thornton & Ocasio, 1999, p. 804). This social reality can be influenced by many different factors, such as religion, industry characteristics, and actors involved in the formation of logics (Gümüsay et al., 2020). For example, in the banking sector, the development of the banking or financial sector is strictly governed by banks in cooperation with state institutions (Almandoz, 2014). Lack of constitutive legitimacy significantly impacts how conflicting institutional logics are (Boone & Özcan, 2020). Religion has been conceptualised from an institutional perspective in relation to the beliefs being rooted in traditions and rituals that shape formal organisations, such as churches (Creed et al., 2010). With such institutions, market and religion logics are often in conflict because of the differences in their purpose, products, and practices (Thornton et al., 2012). For example, the payment of interest is banned in the Islamic banking system (Quran, 2, 275), which fundamentally contradicts the orthodox Western banking system (Gümüsay et al., 2020). This is a situation which can then have interesting implications for those destinations and organisations seeking to embrace Islamic-friendly business practices given that it may be that while some visible elements of what is halal (allowed) are followed, such as food, other elements that are haram (forbidden), such as loans from financial organisations that charge interest or acceptance of interest-charging credit cards, may be hidden (Hall & Prayag, 2020).

The existing literature on the institutional environment focuses on how organisations deal with competing or incompatible institutional logics in different markets (Cheung et al., 2020; Faulconbridge & Muzio, 2016; Ramus et al., 2016; Thornton, 2002). For example, Thornton (2002) found that one logic usually dominates and influences the way organisations adapt and change according to institutional pressures. Faulconbridge and Muzio (2016) have found that organisations can employ several tactics to adapt their organisational practices to deal with competing institutional logics. This incompatibility makes it more challenging to analyse institutional logics and organisational responses to them.

Organisational responses to institutional logics are influenced by institutions, and their enforcement mechanisms are formed by government requirements (Peters, 2012). Organisations operate in multiple markets, and they must deal with different layers of institutional environment in these markets (Luo & Zhang, 2016; Meyer & Höllerer, 2014, 2016). The government forms laws and regulations, but the government and other key actors also influence the ways these institutions and their enforcement mechanisms are implemented (Hall, 2009; Boddewyn, 2016). Therefore, the relationship with home and host governments at different levels are important. These relations are dynamic and can be risky, depending on the geopolitics of the countries involved (Dang et al., 2020). This makes the analysis of competing for institutional logics challenging because of the involvement of different actors whose interests may not align.

Ramus et al. (2016) suggest that collaboration is necessary for managing a highly unstable institutional environment, and that collaboration is achieved by formalising standard procedures. Organisations that employ collaboration tend to strictly follow established regulations because they are more visible in a market. Strong visibility encourages organisations to collaborate with different actors to balance their different interests and expectations (Scholz & Wang, 2006).

In contrast, Oliver (1991) found that manipulation is a purposeful strategy that organisations employ to influence and control institutional pressures. To control these pressures, organisations attempt to exercise power over the stakeholders who created them (Cheung et al., 2020). Manipulation is useful when the institutional environment is rather weak or when governments are unwilling or hesitant to intervene because organisations are able to change existing norms and regulations (Pache & Santos, 2010) and which can therefore allow organisations to deal with competing institutional logics (Pache & Santos, 2010). Overt examples of manipulation in tourism include greenwashing, in which businesses claim their products are environmentally friendly or otherwise manipulate their reporting in order to maintain their legitimacy (Thomas, 2014; Guix et al., 2018; Usmani et al., 2020) or the manipulation of online reviews (Gössling et al., 2018; Gössling et al., 2019).

Engaging in actor-specific manipulation (Kostova et al., 2008) can help organisations to handle domestic institutional complexity. The central government has the authority to change existing legislation and regulations (Wang et al., 2018, 2020). In some cases, similar legislative powers in some policy areas will also lie with regional governments. Therefore, it is in the interest of an organisation to submit to the requirements of the government or be willing to otherwise contest and influence them (see Box 3.2). By doing so, organisations inevitably seek to manipulate the government to adjust necessary regulations in their favour. Depending on the relative powers of different levels of government within countries, regional and local governments may have only limited regulatory responsibilities (Baranov et al., 2015; Gel'man & Ryzhenkov, 2011). However, regional and local government can sometimes promote a certain regulatory change by bargaining on behalf of organisations.

One response to domestic institutional complexity and issues of compliance is avoidance. Avoidance is a concept proposed by Oliver (1991) as a response to institutional pressures, and suggests that organisations hide their non-conformity to the rules and/or escape the unstable institutional environment. Further, Pache and Santos (2010) contend that when organisations are faced with conflicting institutional demands, they resort to avoidance by concealing their non-compliance and engaging in ceremonial compliance.

BOX 3.2 LEGISLATIVE AND POLICY DISRUPTION

The platform economy is often regarded as a form of disruptive innovation (Hall & Williams, 2020). Much of the disruption is not just to competitors and industry sectors but also in terms of policy, legislation, and regulation. Policy and regulative disruption, as in the well-recognised cases of Airbnb and Uber, can result from conscious choices by businesses to exploit legal loopholes or to challenge regulatory protections for incumbents. The platform economy is only the latest in a series of "disruptive innovations" such as the advent of the new communication technologies, the growth of hospitality franchising over independent food service providers, or the emergence of the car-based suburban mall and big-box stores and their impact on high street shopping. However, many such disruptive innovations can often be accommodated within existing law, such as land use law in the case of shopping malls.

Policy and regulation, e.g. permitting, monitoring, standard setting, compliance, and enforcement, are usually related to the business model of the regulated industry. When business models change, for example, because of the application of new technologies, the result can be a disjunction between the regulatory system and the industry that is being regulated, which is therefore a policy disruption. The policy problem stems from the

> Disconnect between the existing regulatory structure and the business innovation threatening the incumbent industry firms. Moreover, the relevant regulatory structure need not be confined to the regime governing the incumbent industry, as the business innovation might be so novel compared to industry incumbents that it raises policy concerns that the incumbents do not.
>
> (Biber et al., 2017, pp. 1580–81)

Biber et al. (2017) identify four primary types of policy disruption:

- *End-runs* – conscious choices by entrepreneurs to exploit ambiguous legislation and regulation;
- *Exemptions* – express legislative and regulatory loopholes;
- *Gaps* – innovations to which the existing regulatory regime does not apply; and
- *Solutions* – solve problems that regulatory systems are designed to address.

In responding to these disruptions, policymakers have several regulatory responses: using existing regulations to block the new business; not changing the existing regulatory structure; applying existing regulations, and developing new regulations. These responses are outlined in Table 3.1 in the case of Uber and Airbnb (Hall & Williams, 2020).

Source: Hall and Williams (2020)

Table 3.1 Regulatory responses to disruptive innovation

Regulatory tool	Strategy	Application to Uber	Application to Airbnb
Block new business model	Interpret legal rules to block the new business model and preserve existing regulatory and business models.	Only licensed taxis can serve this market. Uber is not permitted to operate at all.	Only licensed accommodation providers can serve this market. Airbnb providers are not legally permitted to operate at all.
No change/"Free pass"	Allow business innovation to proceed without changing the regulatory structure. This may potentially make the previous business model and its associated regulatory structure extinct.	Uber is permitted to serve this market. Existing legal rules for taxis only apply to taxis. Uber remains cheaper than taxis. The value of a taxi license plummets, and the taxi licensing system eventually disappears.	Airbnb providers are permitted to serve this market. Existing legal rules for accommodation providers only apply to providers over a certain room size or open for specific periods. Airbnb remains cheaper than hotels leading to cost pressures on formal accommodation providers and increased pressure to change the accommodation laws.

(*Continued*)

Table 3.1 Continued

Regulatory tool	Strategy	Application to Uber	Application to Airbnb
Old Regulations	Allow the new firm to enter the market but apply existing legal rules. This approach imposes additional regulatory costs on new business models but aims for a "level playing field" between incumbents and innovators.	Existing safety rules for taxi vehicles and taxi drivers are designed to protect customers' safety. Uber is like a taxi. Therefore, existing safety rules for vehicles and drivers apply to Uber just as they do for taxis, increasing the cost of Uber but not blocking market entry.	Existing health and safety regulations for accommodation providers are designed to protect guest safety. An Airbnb provider is like a licensed accommodation provider; therefore, these rules will be applied to Airbnb hosts. This was increasing the cost for hosts but does not block market entry.
New Regulations	Develop new regulatory structures and legal and policy categories. The new regulations need not be neutral between incumbents and innovators.	End the previous licensing system for taxi drivers and vehicles. Adopt new legal rules that address policy concerns such as safety, privacy, employment law, competition, or environmental harm.	A new set of regulations for accommodation providers is developed. These address public and policy concerns such as guest safety, tax rating, health and building regulations, zoning regulations, and environmental harm.

Source: After Biber et al., 2017; Hall & Williams, 2020.

This flexibility in interpreting laws makes the institutional environment more challenging, as formal institutions are not unified (Greenwood et al., 2011). The lack of unified institutions encourages organisations to rely on their networks (Helmke & Levitsky, 2004). Because the government can, in some circumstances, manage organisational non-compliance with regulations, reliance on informal institutions can become dysfunctional (Puffer et al., 2016; Raaijmakers et al., 2015). As a result, MNEs strive to reduce their collaboration with the government at a layer that is necessary.

Being less visible enables organisations to be more flexible in how they respond to institutional ineffectiveness (Greenwood et al., 2011; Meyer & Höllerer, 2016). When the institutional environment is unstable, organisations adapt their processes to address external institutional pressures (Selznick, 1957). Conflicting institutional logics can make the institutional environment highly complex to operate in because organisations must meet different stakeholder demands (Ingstrup et al., 2020; Saka-Helmhout et al., 2016). The experience of dealing with conflicting institutions can serve as a learning mechanism for handling unstable institutional environments (Marano & Kostova, 2016; Ramus et al., 2016). The convergence and divergence of institutional logics can lead to alignment and misalignment at three levels: actor-type, relationship, and system levels. These levels will differ within and between different stakeholders such as governments and organisations (Ingstrup et al., 2020).

Effectiveness of institutions and their enforcement

The effectiveness of formal and informal institutions is an important part of the development of the institutional environment (Garrone et al., 2019; Helmke & Levitsky, 2004). Their effectiveness is measured by the extent to which formal rules and procedures are enforced and obeyed (Helmke & Levitsky, 2004). Rules and regulations are more tangible and concrete, which makes it easier to analyse their effectiveness. Informal institutions are not as concrete as formal ones (North, 1990), which makes it more challenging to analyse their enforcement and effectiveness (Tsai, 2006).

Formal institutions, such as rules and regulations, are more tangible because they are written and have boundaries (North, 1990). These boundaries are effective if the rules and regulations are properly enforced (Malesky & Taussig, 2017). The boundaries are formed as a result of creating the institutional environment, which is influenced by the relationship between key actors (Besharov & Smith, 2014). These key actors, such as government at different levels, guide the creation and enforcement of formal institutions depending on the state's governance structure (Peters, 2012). However, enforcement mechanisms and punishment for non-compliance can be costly for the government (Malesky & Taussig, 2017), particularly in terms of public perceptions. Hence, different actors can manipulate the interpretation of these institutions and their boundaries (Brinks, 2003; Tsai, 2006) and have a guiding role in developing the institutional environment, which can be driven informally (Azari & Smith, 2012).

A combined national system of institutions helps shape and guide the strategic behaviour of different actors (Ahmadjian, 2016; Paul & Feliciano-Cestero, 2020). The interactions of formal and informal institutions are driven by the effectiveness of their implementation and enforcement (Helmke & Levitsky, 2004). Previous examinations of interactions between institutions have focused on informal institutions being complementary, accommodating, substitutive, or competing, based on their effectiveness. However, the degree of effectiveness of the institutional system is important but oversimplified when studying the institutional environment and its various elements. Yet, the different interactions can enable an understanding of the complexity of the institutional environment and how organisations handle it (Poulis & Poulis, 2016). Examining the configurations of the interaction between formal and informal institutions can help identify patterns that tourism and hospitality organisations use to navigate different institutional environments. Nevertheless, the applicability of institutional effectiveness will differ depending on organisational attributes and positioning in the field (Greenwood et al., 2011).

Legitimation

Legitimation is a process of gaining social acceptance and normalising acts and behaviours (Zelditch, 2001). The government can affect the legitimation process by interfering in organisational decision-making (Bitektine & Haack, 2015; Deephouse, 1996; Kujala et al., 2020), as well as investment options (Gorynia et al., 2019). The public is a stakeholder that is fundamental to the legitimation process via social judgements (Deephouse et al., 2017). Indeed, for many commentators, legitimation is equated with public legitimation, although the governmental influence on the reputations of an organisation is also an important factor that can affect the legitimacy process (Bitektine, 2011; Suchman, 1995). Organisational attributes, such as positioning in the field, performance, and institutional knowledge, can also affect how organisations deal with the institutional environment and legitimation process (Dau, 2016; Greenwood et al., 2011; Kostova et al., 2008; Luo et al., 2017) and can help organisations access financial resources and networks (Deephouse,

1996; Meyer & Scott, 1983; Rottig, 2016), and develop organisational capabilities (Gölgeci et al., 2019). All of these attributes therefore enable organisations to strengthen their financial position in the market and establish the necessary networks to navigate the institutional environment (Rottig, 2016).

Increased visibility, for example, via campaigns and networking, can help organisations gain more attention at the government level. This often leads to their accessing strategic resources (Boddewyn & Brewer, 1994; Murtha & Lenway, 1994; Tost, 2011). Strategic positioning is also partly determined by an organisation's strategic importance to a country's or destination's economic development and the sector in which it operates.

Organisational attributes can also influence a firm's ability to gain external legitimacy (Caussat et al., 2019; Kostova & Zaheer, 1999). The attributes include an organisation's size, performance, and reputation (Deephouse, 1996; Kostova & Zaheer, 1999; Tost, 2011). Tost (2011) argues that size is directly linked to market visibility and affects different stakeholders' perceptions. Such perceptions can significantly impact the judgement process, which is crucial to legitimation.

Organisational performance is another factor affecting an organisation's legitimation. Performance is commonly measured by financial metrics but can also include consumer metrics as well. Deephouse (1996), for example, found that organisational performance can be endorsed by regulators. Drori and Honig (2013) extend this perspective by suggesting that legitimacy can be endorsed by those in authority, while the public is increasingly seen as a source of endorsement of organisational activity, especially with respect to positive perception about an organisation (Deephouse et al., 2017). Regardless, the process of endorsement is a conscious act that influences organisational behaviour (Deephouse, 1996). Significantly, in a tourism context, the endorsement has become increasingly tied to various aspects of sustainability, for example, social dimensions such as human rights and treatment of minorities, economic aspects such as labour rights, and various environmental aspects such as animal rights, carbon management, and biodiversity conservation. These aspects of endorsement might be explicitly tied to third party evaluations, e.g. for credentialing purposes, as well as to campaigns from pressure groups. In such cases, actions can have implications for organisational disclosure strategies and management practices (Herold & Lee, 2019). Indeed, the significance of public endorsement as a means of legitimation for organisations means that many tourism organisations and destinations are increasingly becoming a focus for political consumerism (Seyfi & Hall, 2020).

BOX 3.3 BOYCOTTING AND PERFORMANCE

A boycott may be defined as "the refusal and incitement to refusal to have commercial or social dealings with offending groups or individuals" (De Crespigny & McKinnel, 1960, p. 319). Boycotting acts are often tied to collective public expressions of disapproval and protest that are potentially affecting the brand, image, and even commercial viability of the boycott target – a country, destination, government, individual, or firm – and therefore function as a significant factor in legitimation. Boycotts are among the most frequent forms of consumer expression against perceived unethical or egregious acts by firms and corporations (Farah & Newman, 2010). In some circumstances, authorities or pressure groups may urge consumers not to buy specific products or the products of a particular business or destination to encourage the adoption of particular businesses practices (Farah & Newman, 2010; Seyfi & Hall, 2020). This is of growing significance given its potential repercussions on economic performance measures as well as the potential effects on market share and sales and the image of targeted organisations and destinations (Shaheer et al., 2018; Seyfi & Hall, 2020). Interestingly, Delacote (2009) distinguishes between market boycotts and media-oriented boycotts, the aim of the former being to reduce sales and the latter to signal disapproval and to increase public awareness. Clearly, media-oriented boycotts are aimed at delegitimising organisational behaviours, but this may also have the consequence of reducing sales. In a study of 1023 boycott events with 93 targeted firms in Korea during 2006–2016, Yang and Rhee (2020) found that public boycotts positively affected CSR disclosure speed. However, the disclosure speed did also vary depending on the magnitude of the potential loss resulting from failing to act and from simply responding too slowly to such boycotts. Nevertheless, CSR disclosure was found to be a significant risk-reduction mechanism against boycotts, given greater transparency with respect to business policies and actions.

Shaheer et al. (2018) identified 146 destination boycotts that were initiated between 1948 and 2015, with more than 90% of the observed boycotts emerging between 2003 and 2015. They reported four main factors for the increasing number of boycotts over the years: 1) innovation of new technology, specifically social media platforms such as Facebook and Twitter; 2) the increase in social movements; 3) emphasis on ethical consumerism; and 4) the use of tourism as a vehicle for social change. Shaheer et al. (2019) examined the reasons behind tourist boycotts and showed that human rights violations (e.g. unjust treatment and policies towards the LGBT community or other discriminatory practices based on race, gender, and nationality), animal welfare concerns, and political and environmental issues are the most common reasons for destination boycotts.

The form of the relationship between different actors affects the actions organisations take to gain and maintain legitimacy. The relationship is influenced by the interests of these actors. The relationship has a temporal dimension – it develops as a result of the past and has consequences for the future. Temporality is a dynamic process of change and can facilitate examining different stages of change and outcomes (Langley, 1999). The changes in interests between different stakeholders influence their evolving relationship. This relationship is not linear, because, to a degree, the actors involved can change. As a result, the legitimation process also has a significant temporal dimension (Zapata Campos et al., 2018).

The temporality of the relationship between the key stakeholders can influence the legitimation process. The past and future shape an organisation's present actions. Past events and projected future events may thus shape temporal experiences (Deleuze, 1994). Organisations use connections established in the past to develop present relationships with government, non-government organisations, the public, and other relevant actors that can predict the outcomes of their relationships and legitimation processes in the future. The temporal experience is, thus, whether their relationships facilitate or obstruct their ability to gain and maintain legitimacy.

The interests between different actors, change as a result of increasing institutional pressures (Oliver, 1991). Further, different government levels pursue different interests, which makes it more challenging for MNEs to achieve their goals (Hall & Jenkins, 1995; Wang et al., 2018). When the governments' and organisations' interests converge, operating in the complex institutional environment is less challenging for the different actors.

Organisations should submit to existing regulations to receive privileges from the government (Bitektine & Haack, 2015; Deephouse, 1996). Non-compliance with existing regulations can largely affect organisations' legitimation process. They can also try to hide their non-compliance with existing regulations to avoid jeopardising their ability to gain legitimacy. By demonstrating that they submit to regulations, organisations ensure that they still gain privileges, such as financial benefits and tax cuts from the central government, and access to networks in foreign markets from the regional government (Luo et al., 2017; Wang et al., 2020).

Another reason for diverging interests is because MNEs decrease their government dependency by learning how to operate in a highly unstable institutional environment (Zhang & Merchant, 2020). The political science literature emphasises the importance of legitimacy at the macro level because it influences different actors' perceptions of a government and a country (Allee & Huth, 2006; Crook, 1987; McDonough et al., 1986). External stakeholders' negative perceptions are likely to weaken a country's legitimacy (Gilley, 2006). This literature provides evidence that a government's political legitimacy can affect the external legitimacy of MNEs from that country.

Deephouse (1996) and Elsbach and Sutton (1992) state that to gain legitimacy, organisations must satisfy and prioritise the actor whose perception most strongly affects their operations. This is a simplistic assumption, because, while organisations may prioritise whom to satisfy, they do not always have a choice.

When the interest gap between the parties increases, MNEs focus on their core goals of organisational development, and the government focuses on its core goals of economic development of the country and its regions. The government can influence an MNE's image and reputation, which can shape foreign partners' perceptions and judgements – both important factors that affect organisational legitimacy (Bitektine & Haack, 2015).

Networks with different actors can create obstacles for MNEs to gain external legitimacy. An adversarial relationship can do this in the form of sudden institutional changes being introduced that influence the organisational legitimation process. The relationships between organisations and the government at different levels are dynamic, and these companies have the knowledge and experience of managing these relationships. This enables them to capitalise on different relationships with governments at different levels and to engage in a positive legitimation process. Understanding why and how the multi-layered institutional environment evolves can help us to analyse it more rigorously.

BOX 3.4 LEGITIMACY AND INSTITUTIONAL PRESSURES

In their pursuit of legitimacy, organisations modify themselves to be compatible with the characteristics (structures, beliefs, and discourses) of their institutional environments. As a consequence, organisations from the same field will often be structurally and strategically similar as they respond to similar institutional pressures (cognitive, normative, and coercive), resulting in a process known as isomorphism (Deephouse, 1996; Scott, 2008). Soares et al. (2020), for example, in a study of technology adoption in hotels identified signs of isomorphism across a number of technology adoption practices and uses. The found that hoteliers adopted similar standards, felt the need to mimic competition, and strove to be positively evaluated on sites such as TripAdvisor in order to achieve legitimacy in the marketplace. Consumers were perceived as powerful agents driving technology adoption in the sector, although trade associations or other governing bodies appeared to have little influence on technology adoption decisions, with certification from third parties being perceived as a more important source of legitimation than recognition from government bodies or industry associations.

Coercive isomorphism refers to the conformity to certain practices as a result of rules, legislation, or other coercive mechanisms, and economic and regulatory sanctions. Yet, under conditions of uncertainty in a relatively unregulated organisational field, as in the case of sustainability in the tourism industry (Zapata Campos et al., 2018), normative and cognitive aspects of the institutional environment become more salient. Normative isomorphism comes, for example, from unquestioned adherence to industry standards but also prevalent values and preferences in a market or a community. While cognitive isomorphism (or mimesis) refers to the unconscious reproduction of standards, practices, or structures following those who appear to be successful in the organisational field. Nevertheless, organisations within the same field do not always show similar sustainability strategies and practices (Hall et al., 2016; Peters et al., 2020) despite being exposed to common institutional pressures.

Developments in institutional theory show how institutional forces can also lead to heterogeneity in a sector rather than isomorphic homogeneity, given that organisations differ in their receptivity to pressures (Hoffman, 2001). For example, in the case of tourism businesses the power of the department or individual promoting CSR and sustainability practices is an internal aspect that may explain different responses. Delmas and Toffel (2008) also showed how organisations channel institutional pressures through different sub-units, which frame pressures according to their routines. For example, legal departments frame them in terms of risk and liability, while financial departments do it in terms of costs and revenue. The consequence is that sustainability can be differentially framed within the same organisation as a competitiveness strategy, as regulatory pressure, or as an ethical responsibility depending on the section responsible (Bansal & Roth, 2000). Other internal organisational features such as the role of leadership values (Egri & Herman, 2000), managerial attitudes (Cordano & Frieze, 2000; Sharma, 2000), and historical environmental performance can also influence how managers perceive stakeholder pressures and their responses (Prakash, 2000), and the visibility of the firm. In addition, Zapata Campos et al. (2018) noted the differentials between public pressure on company environmental performance in the destination and tourist generating countries as being a potential factor in firm actions. Therefore, differences in the adoption of sustainable tourism practices reflect not only different levels of institutional pressures but also differences in organisational characteristics, since internal organisational dynamics, including for those that operate internationally, act as moderating factors that magnify or diminish the influence of institutional pressures.

Oliver (1991) highlights that organisations respond to their institutional environments in different ways, varying from compliance, compromise, and avoidance, to defiance and manipulation (Table 3.2). One of the possible responses is what has been termed "decoupling" (Meyer & Rowan, 1977), which refers to the process whereby organisations "that adopt particular structures or procedures may opt to respond in a ceremonial manner, making changes in their formal structures to signal conformity but then buffering internal units, allowing them to operate independent of these pressures" (Scott, 2008, p. 171). The term has also been used to refer to implementation gaps in sustainability standards (Bromley & Powell, 2012; Jamali, 2010; Zapata Campos et al., 2018). Yet, beyond the decoupling explanation, CSR and sustainability reports and codes of conduct, although taken initially as ceremonial conformity, can turn performative and become effective over time with real consequences (Bartley & Zhang, 2012), especially as external stakeholders start to use the data in such reports opening it to greater scrutiny. For example, in their case study of the Swedish travel operator Apollo, Zapata Campos et al. (2018, p. 15) suggest,

> Since the risk for buffering is high in a lowly regulated sector with few specific resources allocated to monitoring gaps between

Table 3.2 Strategic responses to institutional pressures

Strategies	Tactics	Examples
Acquiesce	Habit	Follow taken-for-granted institutional norms and practices
	Imitation	Copy and mimic institutional models
	Compliance	Obey rules and accept norms and practices
Compromise	Balance	Balance the expectations of multiple actors and stakeholders
	Pacification	Placate and accommodate institutional actors and elements
	Bargain	Negotiate with institutional constituents and stakeholders
Avoid	Conceal	Disguise non-conformity
	Buffer	Loosen institutional attachments
	Escape	Change goals, activities or domains
Defy	Dismiss	Ignore explicit institutional norms, mores, and values
	Challenge	Contest institutional rules and requirements
	Attack	Assault the sources of institutional pressure
Manipulate	Co-option	Cooperate with influential agencies, constituents, and stakeholders
	Influence	Seek to shape institutional values, rules, and criteria
	Control	Seek to dominate institutional constituents, stakeholders and processes

Source: After Oliver (1991), Zapta Campos et al., 2018.

voluntary standards and practices, the role of NGOs and the media in exposing non-implementation or fulfilment of standards is crucial.

Ceremonially adopted rules can therefore lead to change over time and recouple formal and informal structures as a consequence of reflexivity and negotiations that convince internal organisational actors of their appropriateness independent of instrumental considerations (Dashwood, 2012). Internal and external debates of sustainability and responsibility may, therefore, also create conditions for future change through organisational learning (Dashwood, 2012, 2014), an issue that may be critical for the inclusion of various factors such as sustainability data in CSR discourses (Parker & Chung, 2018).

Source: Adapted from Zapata Campos et al. (2018)

Governance

Governance is the act of governing (Hall, 2011a). Governance has emerged as a significant theme in tourism studies, especially in the planning and policy-related literature, and is often used interchangeably with the study of government and the state. There is no single, accepted definition of governance. This is reflected in Kooiman's (2003, p. 4) concept of governance as "the totality of theoretical conceptions on governing". Definitions tend to suggest recognition of a change in political practices involving, amongst other things, increasing globalisation, the rise of networks that cross the public–private divide, the marketisation of the state, and increasing institutional fragmentation (Pierre, 2000, 2009a; Pierre & Peters, 2000, 2005; Amore & Hall, 2016, 2017). Three broad, and often overlapping, meanings of governance can now be identified in the tourism and wider social science literature (Figure 3.2). First, it is used to describe contemporary state

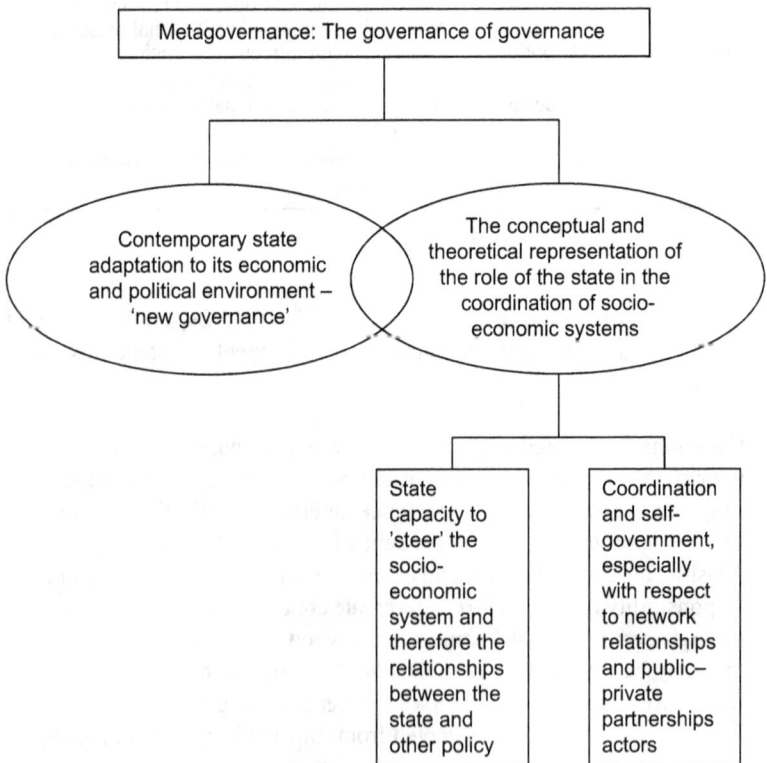

Figure 3.2 The meanings of governance.

adaptation to its economic and political environment with respect to how it operates. This is often referred to as 'new governance', and although this categorisation is justifiably criticised (Treib et al., 2007), it has become a widely used term. Yee (2004, p. 487) provided a very basic definition of this approach by describing new modes of governance as "new governing activities that do not occur solely through governments". This approach to governance includes private actors being heavily involved in policy formulation, something which is very common in tourism, for example, and/or public actors being only marginally based on regulative powers or not based on regulation at all. Deriving mainly from the European and Antipodean experience, Hall (2011a) identified six main elements of the new modes of governance approach: participation and power-sharing, multi-level integration, diversity and decentralisation, deliberation, flexibility and revisability, and experimentation and knowledge creation and transfer.

The second broad meaning of governance is that it is used to denote a conceptual and theoretical representation of the role of the state in the coordination of socio-economic systems. However, it should be noted that the two approaches to governance are not mutually exclusive as the use of the term "governance" as a form of shorthand for new forms of governance in Western societies is itself predicated on particular conceptions of what the role of the state should be in contemporary society and of the desirability and nature of state intervention. This second meaning can therefore, in turn, be divided into two further categories (Pierre & Peters, 2000). The first focuses on the capacity of the central state to "steer" the socio-economic system and therefore the relationships between the central state and other policy actors (Pierre & Peters, 2000). This notion of steering has come to reflect increasingly complex institutional and actor environment that the central state finds itself in as a result of globalisation and (pre-COVID-19) shifts in politics and political administration thinking (new public management) that served to reduce or "hollow out" the role of the central state. The second focuses on coordination and self-government, especially with respect to network relationships and public–private partnerships (Rhodes, 1997).

Meta-governance is simultaneously both a critical approach to the study of governance and a way of thinking about how governance is structured and applied (Amore & Hall, 2016, 2017). As a result, meta-governance reflects the idea that government interventions and policies are reflections of theories (Pierre & Peters, 2000). In the case of governance, such often implicit theories usually cover both theories of the role of the state and the proper actions of government and theories of social interaction and change in social, economic, and political systems. Conceptualised as "the governance of governance" (Jessop, 2011, p. 106), meta-governance explicitly questions the values, norms, principles, and paradigms/ideologies that underpin governance systems and governing approaches (Kooiman & Jentoft, 2009). This includes the assumptions that shape the application and promotion of different forms of intervention (Hall, 2016b), and how political authorities promote and guide the "self-organisation of governance systems through the 'rules of the game', organizational knowledge, institutional tactics and other political strategies" (Jessop, 1997, p. 575).

In terms of different approaches to interventions and policies, a typology of governance can help illustrate the relationship between substance and process. Drawing on the work of Pierre and Peters (2000), among others, Hall (2011a) developed a typology of four governance types applied in a tourism context. Each of the conceptualisations of governance structures is related to the use of particular sets of policy instruments and their implementation (Figure 3.3). Critical to the different modes of governance are the relationships that exist between public and private policy actors and the steering modes that range from hierarchical top-down steering to non-hierarchical approaches. The main elements of the four models or frameworks of governance are outlined in Table 3.3, which identifies their main characteristics, the policy instruments associated with each concept of governance, and various dimensions with respect to policymaking and implementation. These were subsequently applied by Hall (2016b) to help explain the application of different types of behavioural interventions in a sustainability and tourism context. However, it should be emphasised that such a typology is

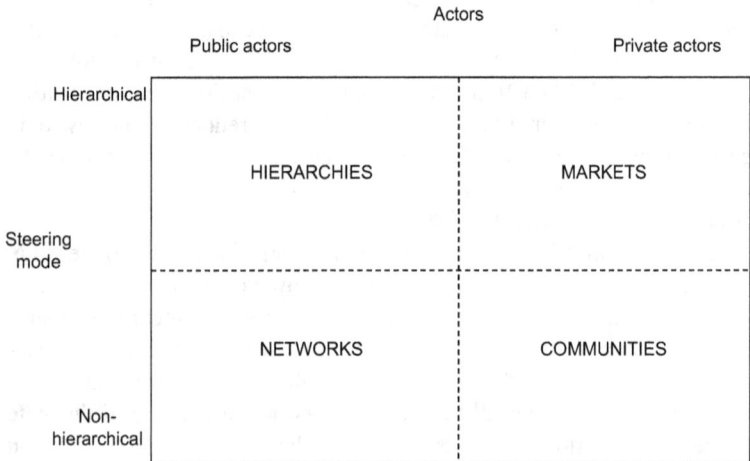

Figure 3.3 Frameworks of governance typology.

Table 3.3 Frameworks of governance and their characteristics

	Hierarchies	Communities	Networks	Markets
Classificatory type characteristics	– Idealised model of democratic government and public administration – Distinguishes between public and private policy space – Focus on the public or common good – Command and control (i.e. "top-down" decision-making) – Hierarchical relations between different levels of the state	– Notion that communities should resolve their common problems with a minimum of state involvement – Builds on a consensual image of the community and the positive involvement of its members in collective concerns – Governance without government – Fostering of civic spirit	– Facilitate coordination of public and private interests and resource allocation and therefore enhance the efficiency of policy implementation – Range from coherent policy communities/policy triangles through to single-issue coalitions – Regulate and coordinate policy areas according to the preferences of network actors than public policy considerations – Mutual dependence between network and state	– Belief in the market as the most efficient and just resource allocative mechanism – Belief in the empowerment of citizens via their role as consumers – Employment of monetary criteria to measure the efficiency – Policy arena for economic actors where they cooperate to resolve common problems
Governance/policy themes	Hierarchy, control, compliance	Complexity, local autonomy, devolved power, decentralised problem-solving	Networks, multi-level governance, steering, bargaining, exchange and negotiation	Markets, bargaining, exchange and negotiation
Policy standpoint	Top: policymakers; legislators; central government	Bottom: implementers, "street-level bureaucrats" and local officials	Where negotiation and bargaining take place	Where bargaining takes place between consumers and producers

(Continued)

Table 3.3 Continued

	Hierarchies	Communities	Networks	Markets
Underlying model of democracy	Elitist	Participatory	Hybrid/stakeholder, a significant role given to interest groups	Consumer determined; citizen empowerment
Primary focus	Effectiveness: to what extent are policy goals actually met?	What influences action in an issue area?	Bargained interplay between goals set centrally and actor (often local) innovations and constraints	Efficiency: markets will provide the most efficient outcome
View of non-central (initiating) actors	Passive agents or potential impediments	Potentially policy innovators or problem shooters	Tries to account for the behaviour of all those who interact in the development and implementation of policy	Market participants are best suited to "solve" policy problems
Distinction between policy formulation and implementation	Actually and conceptually distinct; policy is made by the top and implemented by the bottom	Blurred distinction: policy is often made and then re-made by individual and institutional policy actors	Policy-action continuum: policymaking and implementation seen as a series of intentions around which bargaining takes place	Policy-action continuum
Criterion of success	When outputs/outcomes are consistent with *a priori* objectives	Achievement of actor (often local) goals.	Difficult to assess objectively, success depends on actor perspectives	Market efficiency
Implementation gaps/deficits	Occur when outputs/ outcomes fall short of *a priori* objectives	"Deficits" are a sign of policy change, not a failure. They are inevitable	All policies are modified as a result of negotiation (there is no benchmark)	Occur when markets are not able to function

	Good ideas poorly executed	Bad ideas faithfully executed	"Deficits" are inevitable as abstract policy ideas are made more concrete	Market failure; inappropriate indicator selection
Reason for implementation gaps/deficits				
Solution to implementation gaps/deficits	Simplify the implementation structure; apply inducements and sanctions	"Deficits" are inevitable	"Deficits" are inevitable	Increase the capacity of the market
Primary policy instruments	– Law – Regulation – Clear allocation and transfers of power between different levels of the state – Development of a clear set of institutional arrangements – Licensing, permits, consents, and standards – Removal of property rights – Development guidelines and strategies that reinforce planning law	– Self-regulation – Public meetings/town hall meetings – Public participation – Non-intervention – voluntary instruments – Information and education – Volunteer associations – Direct democracy (citizens initiated referenda) – Community opinion polling – Capacity building of social capital	– Self-regulation and coordination – Accreditation schemes – Codes of practice – Industry associations – Non-government organisations	– Corporatisation and/or privatisation of state bodies – Use of pricing, subsidies and tax incentives to encourage desired behaviours – Use of regulatory and legal instruments to encourage market efficiencies – Voluntary instruments – Non-intervention – Education and training to influence behaviour

Source: After Hall, 2011a, 2016b.

only a means of simplifying an otherwise complex reality and that the four types of governance identified here should not be regarded as "ideal types".

Are institutions immortal?

Institutions, formal or informal, continuously evolve and are intertwined with the environment that they develop (Shipilov, 2012). This would suggest that institutions are potentially immortal because of the temporal legacy that they carry. However, whether institutions are immortal or not, depending on their historical development and evolution in a larger institutional system. Different stakeholders also impact the development of institutions (Peters, 2012). For example, government change, and as a result this may lead to the restructuring of legislative systems (Kitschelt, 2000; Peters, 2012). This does not mean that institutions disappear, but that they may change. In Russia, the constitution was completely re-written after the collapse of the Soviet Union in 1990; hence, many regulations were also formally re-written, although some were retained (Gel'man, 2015). The government structure may also change, new departments and ministries or constellations of departments and ministries created, which influences the movement of people into different roles within organisations and sectors. For example, in recognition of the international nature and significance of the climate crisis, President Biden appointed former Secretary of State John Kerry to a new position of special presidential envoy for climate

> because of his expertise and experience on the global stage. Biden has repeatedly emphasised that his administration's climate ambition will touch all aspects of government, including national security, public health, foreign relations, economic policy and racial justice. Kerry will be able to implement Biden's plans.
>
> (Reid, 2020)

This means that while formal institutions may be amended or almost completely changed, informal institutions are potentially immortal and influence the evolution of the overall institutional environment.

BOX 3.5 ARE GOVERNMENT ORGANISATIONS IMMORTAL?

In contrast to private sector tourism organisations, where termination is regarded as frequent and widespread, especially with respect to entrepreneurship (e.g. Hall & Rusher, 2004), accounts of public organisations occur in a very different context. The seminal work of Kaufman (1976), for example, posed the question "Are government organizations immortal?" Using a sample of organisations within the "Executive Office of the President" and within US federal departments from 1923 to 1973, Kaufman (1976) found that 27 organisations had been terminated and 294 had been established during this period. Such findings were regarded as supporting the notion that government organisations are immortal, otherwise referred to as the "immortality thesis". Nevertheless, subsequent studies found that Kaufman's research had substantial issues with respect to sampling in terms of both the range of organisations examined and sampling points, for example, not acknowledging organisations established after 1923 but which had been terminated before 1973 (Lewis, 2002; Peters & Hogwood, 1988). Nevertheless, a substantial issue still remains as to what termination means and how change should be assessed.

Assessing change

Assessing the past and future of organisations and institutions necessitates an understanding of temporal analysis: "systematically situating particular moments (including the present) in a temporal sequence of events and processes stretching over extended periods" (Pierson, 2004, p. 2) is essential for understanding change. There are four ideas involved in the notion of change (Kay, 2006):

- an enduring thing;
- its various possible states;
- the identification of an initial and a final state by the temporal index; and
- the characterisation of these states.

A thing's potential to change is limited by the range of possible states admissible for the type set of which it is a member. This is not as abstract as it sounds and is critical for explaining changes in things, such as organisations, and changes in kind (Hall, 2010a). If the thing is tourism policy or its organisational form such as a DMO, for example, only certain states are possible; that is, only certain things can be a tourism policy or organisation. If the boundary is overstepped, the thing (tourism policy) becomes another thing (another policy field – say environment), rather than a different value of the same thing.

However, the identity of the thing through time, the endurance, raises an awkward philosophical question:

> if a changing thing really changes, it cannot literally be one and the same thing before and after the change: however, if a changing thing literally remains one and the same thing (that is, it retains its identity) throughout the change, then it cannot really have changed.
>
> (Kay, 2006, p. 6)

This is not philosophical irrelevance as many debates over public policy, including tourism and its organisation, are debates about things and values that are politically contested. The identity of something over time is even more complex when the thing is composite and in flux, as is often the case of tourism policy and the organisations that implement it. For example, is tourism policy under a Keynesian welfare state a different thing from that under neoliberal tourism policy, or is it a different value of the same thing? (Hall, 2010a). Similarly, tourism may have different industry associations connected to it at different times, but there is usually still a recognisable tourism organisation of some sort (MacCarthaigh, 2012; Zapata & Hall, 2012). Institutions, organisations, and public policy also consist of many processes operating at different speeds. Therefore, it is important to distinguish between the role of events (an abrupt change) with process (a more gradual change) (Hall, 2016a). Much of the focus in research on tourism and change, including organisational and policy dimensions, is often on the role of high-profile high-magnitude events; however, the role of "normal" process is perhaps even more important to understanding changes in policy and organisational states in either composition or time. This is especially so as adaptation and policy learning is something that is often highly valued in tourism. Indeed, in a general public agency setting, Boin et al. (2010, p. 404) observed that with respect to organisational survival, "the name of the game is not design for survival but design for adaptation".

Destination management and marketing organisations have been around for over 50 years, although sometimes in different forms. Since the 1970s, political philosophies with respect to the roles of government, including with respect to tourism, have changed; as a result, DMOs have changed too.

Nevertheless, they still continue to exist in some form in most destinations (Pike & Page, 2014). As Hall and Veer (2016, p. 356) suggest, "So long as they continue to 'do something' and visitor arrivals increase then they are likely to survive". As they argue:

> Providing DMOs are perceived as continuing to attract tourists, they will be regarded as serving a useful role by industry interests as well as other stakeholders. This also includes with respect to the attraction of public funds for tourism promotional and other campaigns that would otherwise not be obtainable to support the industry. If this occurs, then the growth coalitions and tourism interests that formed the DMO will likely continue to advocate its necessity and continuation... the adage that "if there is an increase in visitor numbers it is because of the successful marketing efforts and if there is a decline it is because of unavoidable external factors" certainly seems to apply to most DMOs.
>
> (Hall & Veer, 2016, p. 355)

Interestingly, research suggests that organisational characteristics may actually have relatively little influence on public agency survival (Adam et al., 2007; Lewis, 2002), although the effects of some variables may change over time. In the US, having a committee/board structure increases a public agency's risk of termination initially although after 6.5 years this feature appears to work to the advantage of agency survival. Independence shows a similar pattern. Initially a liability, it becomes an asset for survival after a slightly shorter period (Boin et al., 2010). Nevertheless, as potentially may be expected, there is some evidence that a change of party in government increases the risk of agency termination (Lewis, 2002), while termination also appears less likely when politicians are fiscally constrained and more likely during periods of unified government (Carpenter & Lewis, 2004). There is therefore a suggestion that, rather than economic and technological change being factors in termination, public organisation survival may be connected more to political factors.

Conclusions

This chapter has furthered the discussion on the value of institutional and cognate theories to the understanding of public and private tourism organisations. It began by emphasising the multiple layers of the institutional environment that exist and their importance in understanding organisational behaviour. The various layers are interrelated to the jurisdictional and constitutional structure of individual countries, but all of these, though different, are overlaid by the international sphere, which is extremely important in terms of international tourism and mobility given the wide range of multi-lateral and unilateral agreements that exist.

The chapter then examined different dimensions of the analysis of these multiple institutional layers, including the use of institutional logics, effectiveness, legitimacy, and governance. The chapter then discussed the survival of institutions and organisations, noting especially the question of are government organisations immortal? However, a constant issue that besets institutional analysis is that institutional immortality, like a number of issues in institutional studies in a tourism context, lacks longitudinal and historical analysis. Therefore, in the next concluding chapter, we provide comments on methodological guidance for institutional analysis, and potential future research directions.

4 Conclusions

Methodological issues and future directions in institutional analysis in tourism and hospitality

Introduction

This final chapter provides a brief overview of some of the methodological issues in operationalising institutional theory and offers some potential future research directions for studies in the area. It is structured into three sections. The first provides a brief account of methodological issues involved in 'doing' institutional analysis. The second section provides some thoughts from the authors on future research directions. The final section gives some brief concluding remarks to the book.

Using theory: methodological issues

One of the biggest challenges that students (defined broadly) of tourism face is with respect to 'doing theory'. In other words, how do we apply institutional theory to our understanding of tourism and hospitality? The answer to this is three-fold. First, institutional theory provides us with a valuable means by which to better understand organisations and what they do over time, especially in response to external pressures. Second, it helps us understand the spaces that exist between organisations and the inter-relationships between them. In so doing, it allows for a more critical eye on the development of networks between organisations, especially public–private partnerships, and inter-organisation collaboration. Third, it also provides a focus for theory-building both within tourism and hospitality research and in connecting such research with the wider social sciences.

The institutional environment is complex because of the different levels at which institutions operate, making examination challenging (Kostova et al., 2008). In the previous chapter we examined multi-scaled institutional analysis from the perspectives of institutional logics; effectiveness of institutions and their enforcement; legitimation and governance. In general, institutional theory requires a rigorous application of different methods to effectively examine tourism and hospitality phenomena. Table 4.1 presents an overview of institutional analysis, methods likely to be employed to examine each lens, the main area of analysis and future directions.

Table 4.1 Institutional theory: methods and future directions

Institutional lens	Methods	Main areas of analysis	Future directions
Institutional logics	Case studies supported by qualitative interviews and archival research	Organisational	Contextualisation Longitudinal studies
Effectiveness of institutions and their enforcement	Quantitative surveys and analysis of outputs and metrics, qualitative interviews, ethnography, case studies, archival research	Policy Organisational	Interactions between formal and informal institutions The implementation and enforcement process: • What is the role of different stakeholders in the enforcement process? • How does a change in government affect implementation processes?
Legitimation	Archival research, surveys, case studies, ethnography	Organisational Governmental (all scales)	The legitimation process should be studied from a temporal perspective. Process thinking Longitudinal studies
Governance	Archival research, Case studies, Ethnography (including online) Interviews (with stakeholders and key decision-makers)	Policy, especially with respect to policy actions and interventions	e-governance as an emerging application Relationships between intervention selection and governance model/theory

Institutional logics

The empirical examination of institutional logics has been mostly focused on analysing secondary data by reviewing changes in policies and regulations and how these changes influence organisational behaviour. The most common research method for examining institutional logics is the case study (Almandoz, 2014; Gümüsay et al., 2020), which has long been widely used in tourism and hospitality research (Beeton, 2005; Hall & Page, 2014; De Urioste-Stone et al., 2018). Even though the approach is widely used, case study research has been criticised by political science and sociology scholars because of its inability to rigorously analyse data (Campbell, 1975) and for its exploratory nature, which often leads to unconfirmable results (Xiao & Smith, 2006). However, in the business, marketing, and tourism disciplines, and elsewhere in the social sciences, the case study has been one of the most popular research strategies because it allows for in-depth exploration of the studied phenomena, as well as accounting for contextual nuances and changes over time (Eisenhardt, 1989; Ragin, 1992; Piekkari et al., 2009, 2010; Quintens & Matthyssens, 2010; Welch et al., 2011; Yin, 2003).

In examining institutional logics case studies tend to apply secondary data, such as surveys, historical, and archival, and investigate the organisational response to competing logics. Case study research in tourism often relies on the use of secondary data, but may also include interviews (Xiao & Smith, 2006) (see Box 4.1). This can be explained by the easier access to secondary data that is publicly available via archival research (Liasidou, 2019), whereas access to interviews can be time-consuming (Darbi & Hall, 2014). Furthermore, sharing information about responses to competing institutional logics can entail providing sensitive information (e.g. manipulation as a response to competing logics), which organisations might not be comfortable to share. For the case studies to be rigorous and provide reliable findings, there is a need to use multiple sources, such as secondary data, survey, interviews, and focus groups. This allows the triangulation of data and ensuring data validity (Jick, 1979; Hall, 2011c). Triangulation reduces misinterpretation of the findings, increases confidence in the validity of the findings, and validates the information received from various sources by examining it from different angles (Denzin, 1989; Flick, 1992). Hence, employing multiple methods to examine competing or conflicting logics can provide a more in-depth understating of the development of institutional logics and its impact on organisations, industries, and societies (Czernek, 2017).

BOX 4.1 KEY ISSUES IN THE ELITE INTERVIEW PROCESS

Interviews with "elite" individuals are "a special case of interviewing that focuses on a particular type of interview partner" (Marshall & Rossman, 2010, p. 155). There are specific constraints that interviews with elites, e.g. key decision-makers, politicians, and organisation heads, bring to the research process and that interviewing or studying "up" with respect to class, political, and social status (Gelles, 1974) is different from interviewing or studying "across" or "down" (Smith, 2006). In elite research, information and knowledge flow from the researched to the researcher, and elite interviews can provide data that might not be available elsewhere. Robson (2008) reported the case of an Australian elite who demonstrated knowledge and contributed a lot of useful information to his study of the social context of intuition used in Australian business decision-making. Apparently, this particular elite had been reflecting on the topic long before the researcher went into the field to collect data. Elites are likely to be well placed when it comes to interpreting public documents and also pre-empting information that is not yet in the public domain and may be especially valuable for the purposes of triangulating research data (Marshall & Rossman, 2010).

Darbi and Hall (2014) identified four main issues in undertaking elite interviews: gaining access, developing rapport, and establishing trust during the interview process, power relations and positionality in elite interviews, and ethical issues in elite interviews. Making contact is critical to the whole elite interview process since it holds the key to the rest of the exercise. Both formal and informal networks are important for improving access and introductions and can be leveraged to make contacts. These connections of social and formal networks often act as sponsors. The more influential sponsor a researcher has, the easier the access. In the absence of an available "sponsor", a good starting point in gaining access should be the researcher's own searches of publicly available directories. Interestingly local politicians and organisation heads may feel less threatened by a foreign interviewer as opposed to a local one since image protection is a high priority for a politician, and a foreign interviewer may be less threatening.

Merely arranging an interview does not pass for a successful interview contact. Developing rapport and establishing trust are important ingredients that an interviewer needs in order to get quality information from elites beyond public relations reports or speeches. Consequently, the degree of openness a researcher can get from interviewees becomes an important factor in determining how many personal as opposed to organisational views he or she can get from elite interviews. The location of the interview has also been proposed as one of the possible moderators of the public–private persona of the elite. "Backstage" and informal public places, such as a good coffee shop or bar, may be particularly useful, although the final choice of interview location usually resides with the interviewee. Another issue salient in developing rapport and gaining trust is how to approach the interview process proper. It is important to realise the brief time available and the limited possibilities of getting a repeat interview soon after, so any controversial or threatening questions should be left till late in the interview process.

At the centre of most of the issues and challenges surrounding elite interviews is the twin mediating factors of positionality and power relations between the researcher and the researched. The researched and researcher's personal characteristics such as age, race, professional status, ethnicity, religion, sex, and spoken languages are all potential sources of power imbalance. Status-wise, the prevailing assumption and position is that the power balance is always tilted in favour of the researched. Hall (2011d) agrees with the notion that power relations always exist between an elite and a researcher, who is dependent on that elite to successfully carry out their research. However, he argues that both actors at any point in time exercise some minimal level of power for as long as the actors have to deal with conflicts through negotiation, collaboration, and compliance. The mere fact that an interview has been granted suggests that the interviewer at least retains some power. This notion therefore conceptualises power as a two-way process in which actors in the relationship exercise some minimal influence over each other. The implication of this conceptualisation is that the researcher can adjust positionality along with the insider–outsider continuum depending on what is required at a given point in time in the relationship.

The challenges that elite interviews present have specific ethical dimensions. Elite interviews unlike non-elite interviews have ethical peculiarities which potential researchers must bear in mind. Some of the strategies employed by researchers to gain access, develop rapport, establish trust, or manipulate power relations and positionality may pass for unethical conduct in some circumstances. For example, a researcher had "to masquerade as a tour guide in order to obtain information from various authorities involved in the tourism industry in India" (Smith, 2006, p. 650). In contrast to non-elites, elites are also often wary about what is put on public record since some of the information they provide can be damaging to their influence and offices. Nevertheless, from the perspective of Hall (2011d), there would (must) be a trade-off at some point in the elite research process since achieving "objective" and ethically-apt research through balancing all interests including self, scholarly community, research subjects, and "sponsors" may be counterproductive or even illusionary – as the researcher must decide on which of the varied and conflicting political, cultural, status, economic, or institutional interests their research will serve, given that no institutional and political research is truly "neutral". Indeed, he even somewhat provocatively suggested that in some cases the decisions of university ethics committees may be more geared to legal and institutional concerns than the broader ethical outcomes of research findings, reinforcing that the ethical decision ultimately lies with the researcher.

Source: Adapted from Darbi and Hall (2014).

Effectiveness of institutions and their enforcement

Research on the effectiveness of institutions often focuses on examining regulations because they are relatively easy to measure and quantify. The existing literature on regulations tends to concentrate on issues of property rights, ownership structures, and political institutions (Causevic & Lynch, 2013; Murtha & Lenway, 1994; Yüksel et al., 2012), although there is also some attention given to international institutions (Hall, 2010b). However, compared to other sectors of comparable economic importance, there is only limited research on implementation in a tourism policy context (Dodds, 2007; Hall, 2009; O'Brien, 2010; Zahra, 2010; Dela Santa, 2013; Rodriguez et al., 2014; Hassan et al., 2020). In highly unstable institutional environments, the political burden illustrates the complexity in developing policies for sustainable tourism (Farmaki et al., 2015). There is a huge conflict between the personalisation of political institutions to suit decision-making elites and narrow economic interests and sustainable tourism development (Yasarata et al., 2010). While the effectiveness of policies and regulations has been explored in tourism, their enforcement and development over time lack empirical investigation (Hall, 2010b).

Similar to institutional logics, policies and regulations tend to be the focus when examining institutions and their effectiveness. This is not surprising because policies and regulations can usually be investigated with publicly available data. In qualitative studies, while Western developed methodologies suggest that a researcher should be a neutral tool when in the field (Fontana & Frey, 2005), in developing economies, a researcher becomes more of an active participant in the data collection process (Causevic & Lynch, 2013). When collecting data on politics and tourism, researcher ideologies need to be considered in relation to security and economic matters (Webster & Ivanov, 2016). This would allow for a more considered account of the types of enforcement mechanisms of different institutions and their historical effectiveness (see Box 4.2).

BOX 4.2 CONDUCTING QUALITATIVE RESEARCH IN RUSSIA UNDER SANCTIONS

With the increase of geopolitical tensions due to the imposition of sanctions, the tourism industry has been significantly impacted due to restriction on the mobility of goods, services, and people (Seyfi & Hall, 2020). Earl (2021) reflected on undertaking qualitative research under sanctions in 2014 and 2015, outside of a Western setting, in Russia. She found that sanctions on Russia, made the institutional environment less effective. In particular, regulatory restrictions on people's movement to and from sanctioned countries pushed Russia to quickly review their import policies and regulations, which impacted the economic development of Russia. Furthermore, the traditional "friendly" relationship between Russia and Ukraine impacted the perceptions of travellers about these countries. This influenced the nostalgic views and networks that travellers have had towards these countries. The imposition of sanctions also impacted the data collection process and questions existing methodological developments.

Sanctions can present serious barriers to fieldwork. As Earl (2021) suggests "access to data can also be jeopardised because of the geopolitical conflicts caused by sanctions". While access to data requires skills and practice, sanctions require researchers to adapt their skill sets. "The sanctions imposed on Russia by the US and the EU countries clearly changed the dynamics of the business environment"

(Earl, 2021), with the author concluding that access to the potential participants can be threatened by powerful actors in the field, including the government and businesses. When in the field during the imposition of sanctions, the researcher cannot remain as a neutral tool, as suggested by Western literature. Sanctions instead directly influence the research process, hence making a researcher more embedded into the local context.

Sanctions also change the institutional environment where information and knowledge is shared. The autonomy of the Russian government increases over information sharing and knowledge dissemination, because of the geopolitical issues between sanctioned countries. The control of the knowledge flow can also influence tourism scholarship because of the participants' uncertainty on what information can and cannot be shared.

The government plays an important role in the formation of the institutional environment. The institutional environment and enforcement mechanisms influence the entire research process. This makes the government a powerful actor in tourism industry research, especially in countries where specific permissions or ethics clearances are required for research.

Source: Adapted from Earl (2021).

Legitimation

Similar to institutional logics, the legitimation process has been examined predominantly through case studies, examining how organisations gain legitimacy in home or foreign markets (Zapata & Hall, 2012; Ruhanen & Whitford, 2018). Studies that examine legitimacy or the legitimation process are more contextualised than studies examining institutional logics and effectiveness. In particular, emerging economies have been the subject of inquiry because their institutional environment is often referred to as unstable, which makes the legitimation process more dynamic and complex (Ahlstrom et al., 2008; Huang-Horowitz & Evans, 2020).

The case studies approach allows for taking contextual nuances and applying them in the analysis (Yin, 2003). Method contextualisation is not common in tourism; however, it can provide opportunities for deeper knowledge generation (Hall, 2011c). Contextualisation of methods can occur at different phases of the research process: formation of the research problem, data analysis, data interpretation, and reporting findings (Tsai, 2006). This allows researchers to account for the different contexts where the legitimation process occurs.

BOX 4.3 THE SPACES OF FIELDWORK

"Fieldwork is a structured temporal and geographical space marked by empirical research on a selected set of subjects" (Hall, 2011e, p. 315). Hall (2011f) identifies six different types of interrelated spaces for fieldwork: temporal space, physical space, regulatory/political space, ethical space, social space, and theoretical/methodological space. This position reflects Lorenz-Meyer's (2004) consideration that physical and social location systematically shapes what we know, and how, given that knowledge is always relative to a particular perspective or stand-point, some of which have been imposed on the viewer. Lorenz-Meyer (2004) also stresses that structurally a location is marked by parameters of social inequality such as gender, race, class, religion, sexuality, and geopolitical location, and their attending subject positions of identity, material conditions, privileges, and emotions. However, as Hall (2011f) emphasises, these spaces are not mutually exclusive and instead over-lap and interact with one another over time.

Temporal space: Fieldwork occurs as part of a wider defined research project that has its own beginning and end, although the implications of the fieldwork can be ongoing, allowing for substantial recollection and review.

Physical space: The field is a physical or virtual space with its own difficulties and challenges, such as access and health and safety issues. The boundary making and drawing which is critical to the suc-cessful undertaking of a research project will usually have a physical component, while university research and ethics committees, fund-ing bodies, and, in some cases, government agencies usually require locational information, even if a virtual location (Hall, 2011d). The location of research is also a significant factor influencing whether research will be supported and/or permitted by universities, sponsors, and governments, as many institutions conduct a risk assessment of locations for insurance and health and safety reasons as well as the sensitivity associated with topics (Kovats-Bernat, 2002; Johansson, 2015; Kloß, 2017).

Regulatory/political space: Rather than being just apoliti-cal spaces, field locations can also be conceptualised as political locations. Locations are positionings in time and space which have specific effects and consequences, and "politics" (Kovats-Bernat, 2002; Lorenz-Meyer, 2004). Fieldwork is subject to regulation and the exercising of power within the relations between fieldworkers and subjects, informants, and gatekeepers, within the institutions of both the researcher and the subjects of research, while many countries require special visas and/or permissions if research is being undertaken (Hall, 2011d; Darbi & Hall, 2014). Such organisations often have guidelines as to what can and cannot be undertaken during fieldwork; this affects not only relations with subjects, but also the selection of methods, questions that can be asked, protocols that must or should be followed, and even where research should or must occur (Engel et al., 2015). Significantly, the role of institutional and actor power and influence on fieldwork topic, design, conduct, and reporting need not be done via formal regulatory structures, but by key actors in gatekeeper organisations using informal means and pressures.

Ethical space: Ethical space occurs at the intersection between regulatory, social, and theoretical spaces, and includes both the formal and informal ethics generated by institutions and their cultures, as well as the personal ethics of the researcher. Ethics here is more than the framework of codes of conduct and what university ethics committees, sponsors, and government agencies agree is permissible before research commences. Meta-ethical issues include consideration of even the "right" to undertake research on particular topics – and in particular locations with particular subjects and methods – as well as consideration of how the results will be used (Hall, 2011d).

Social space: Social experiences and relations in the field can have a profound effect on researchers as working with and observing people is clearly a social experience that may be rich in social relations. Gillen (2011) highlights that the melding of personal and professional roles in participant and ethnographic fieldwork makes for messy, qualitative experiences that are at odds with how social science fieldwork is normatively portrayed. As well as being research journeys undertaking fieldwork is also often a social and emotional journey as well.

Theoretical/methodological space: Fieldwork also occupies a theoretical and methodological space that serves to frame the experiences of the field and help understand them and how research problems are defined and negotiated. As Hall (2011f) argues, the theoretical lens that is applied before, during, and after being in the field, even if multiple in scope, affects what is left in and what is taken out, ignored, or looked for (sometimes even not seen).

Governance

Governance can be examined via a range of qualitative and quantitative methods. Archival and policy studies can, for example, identify the relative application of funds to different areas, the partnerships involved, as well as the responsible agencies. These can also be examined over time so as to provide an account of changes in governance in a temporal context. This can illustrate, for example, how changes in government affect the relative allocation of resources to different policy areas and agencies. In some cases, as noted in Chapter 3, agencies may be transformed or be abolished, also reflecting relative priorities. Such studies can therefore provide rich information on how governance is conducted (Zapata & Hall, 2012; Presenza et al., 2013; Amore & Hall, 2016, 2017; Riensche et al., 2019).

The most common focus of most contributions to the governance debate in institutional and public policy terms is "the role of the state in society" (Pierre, 2000b, p. 4). Therefore, the core concept in governance in institutional and public policy terms, including with respect to policy interventions that seek to make change, is the relationship between state intervention/public authority and societal autonomy or self-regulation (Treib et al., 2007). However, as noted in Chapter 1, there are a number of different approaches to institutional theory, each with their own relative emphasis on the structure – agency debate with respect to human behaviour and society. Case Studies have long been a major research frame used to explain governance, and these have often sought to integrate more agency-oriented work with macro-level structural data. Giddens' (1994) notion of structuration which sought to bring the two levels of analysis together in his work, described agency research as a more "interpretive" form of analysis in which social activity shapes the productive capacities of people and which is marked by the use of qualitative methods such as ethnography. From a methodological perspective, grounded theory has also been utilised as a means of understanding people's experience of both structure and agency, especially in an organisational context (Glaser, 1992), and has been widely applied in tourism and hospitality research (Hardy, 2005; Mehmetoglu & Altinay, 2006; Kornilaki & Font, 2019).

Yet both research as well as the effects that institutions have in terms of policy and state intervention does not occur atheoretically. Researchers use theoretical frames as a means of explaining the world around them, while decision-makers hold assumptions, "policies as theories" as noted in Chapter 1, that help them decide what intervention to select and make them an appropriate subject to study with respect to both organisational processes and their impacts. Rothschild (1999, p. 34) recognised the interconnections between the selection of interventions and public policy philosophy noting that: "Democratic societies have an ongoing concern with the balance of free choice and externalities", and argued that the relationships between political philosophies and the selection of interventions would depend on:

- the externalities predicted to result from behaviour;
- the relative balance between the rights of the individual and those of the state;
- the relative locus of power of the various persons such as civil servants, non-profit administrators, legislators, and/or private sector managers who attempt to direct the behaviour of individuals for the good of society (as defined by the managers, the leaders, and/or the constituents of the society); and
- the relative homogeneity of communities.

Box 4.4 provides a relatively amusing way of describing the nature of these interventions drawn from behavioural economics and social marketing. However, Table 4.2 provides a more detailed account of the inter-relationships between approaches to consumer change, the relative focus on agency (individuals) and structure (society, institutions), how individual decision-making and consumption is primarily understood, the tools that may be used to achieve policy decisions, and the mode of governance to which these are interconnected (Hall, 2014). Significantly the table also highlights how institutional theory may serve to help shed light on individual decision-making actions given the ways in which the framing and doing decision-making are deeply interrelated. The three different approaches to behaviour change in Table 4.2 have different sets of assumptions and work within different paradigmatic frames, even though they all deal with institutions in one way or another. Acknowledging these assumptions may in itself be useful for understanding state interventions, organisational and management processes, and decision-making. However, it is also important to recognise that the different approaches are also intimately related to different understandings of governance, the role of the state, policy learning and change, and the role of different institutions.

Table 4.2 Approaches to consumer change

Approach	Scale	Understanding of individual decision-making	Consumer behaviour is …	Indicative interventions	Dominant mode of governance
Utilitarian	Individual (focus on agency)	Cognitive information processing on the basis of rational utility-maximisation	The means for increasing utility	Labelling, tax incentives, pricing, education, self-regulation	Markets (marketisation and privatisation of state instruments)
Social & psychological (Behavioural economics/ nudging/social marketing)	Individual (focus on the agency but with some acknowledgement of structure but agency is given primacy)	Response to psychological needs, behaviour and social contexts; Dominant paradigm of "ABC": attitude, behaviour, and choice	Satisfier of psychological needs; cultural differentiator; a marker of social meaning and identity	Nudging –making better choices through manipulating a consumer's environment; Social individual and community-based marketing for behavioural change	Markets (marketisation and privatisation of state instruments); Networks (public–private partnerships)
Systems of provision/ Institutions	Community, society, network (focus on the structure)	Constrained/shaped by socio-technical infrastructure and institutions	Routine habit, inconspicuous rather than conspicuous	Short-supply chains, relocalisation; Change more likely to occur because of responses to external activism	Hierarchies (nation-state and supranational institutions); Communities (public–private partnerships, communities)

Source: After Hall 2014.

BOX 4.4 LESSONS, HUGS, SHOVES, NUDGES, OR SMACKS?

These terms are used to describe a range of government mechanisms used to encourage individual and organisational behavioural change (Thaler & Sunstein, 2008; Triggle, 2013; Hall, 2014):

Lesson – The provision of information with respect to a certain behaviour and its externalities in the belief that individuals will change in their own self-interest.

Hug – Covers a wide range of incentives, although these are not usually directly financial, including tax rebates, vouchers, or discounts. For example, in encouraging the adoption of energy-efficient technologies, travelling by active or public transport, or participating in certain recreational and leisure activities.

Nudges – Based on the idea that behaviour can be changed voluntarily without using compulsion. Can include enticing people to take up activities by using financial or time incentives or disincentives or the use of social marketing. For example, stressing social norms or desired social status may encourage people to change behaviour because they want to be perceived in a particular way or think of themselves in a certain way, or using timed price ticketing to encourage access to locations at certain times of the day and not others so as to smooth demand.

Shove – More deliberate than a nudge and is a mildly regulatory approach. For example, some planning departments may restrict certain activities and businesses in some locations but not ban the activity altogether. For example, this may be by the use of zoning powers or other regulatory powers to ban fast-food restaurants near schools, the deliberate location of casinos to minimise social impacts, or private residences being run as Airbnbs.

Smack – The most coercive of all government regulatory measures by banning something outright. Often applied to so-called sin goods and services such as alcohol and drugs and the sex industry, but in some countries it can also apply to what is regarded as appropriate to wear in public, especially for women, and relationships between consenting adults.

Future research directions

Although institutional theory is starting to become well established in tourism and hospitality research, there is a need to move beyond rigour and transparency in case study research, as important as they are (Elsahn et al., 2020). There is a need for greater in-depth knowledge of the studied phenomenon that has been developed and analysed over time (Adie et al., 2020; Sæþórsdóttir & Hall, 2021). To examine organisational responses to institutional logics, we suggest scholars seek to employ a greater use of longitudinal studies, although we readily acknowledge the funding and other difficulties that emerge in such research. This would enable greater exploration of the process of evolution in institutional logics, which is important because this process can help us to understand how the tourism industry has evolved and how organisations experience co-evolution, both together and in relation to the wider institutional context over time. Past events of change shape organisational experience and lead to future behaviour, which is an indication of temporal dimensions in institutional logics (Deleuze, 1994), and can provide important pointers to future industry, community, and destination development, including potentially with respect to resilience (Hall et al., 2017).

Future research should also examine legitimation processes; ideally this would also be complemented by employing longitudinal studies. Many case studies focus on building legitimacy through the lens of organisational identity or reputation (Huang-Horowitz & Evans, 2020; Rao, 1994); however, it is problematic to examine the "process" without looking at the events in the institutional environment that trigger this process (Hernes, 2014). Examining the legitimation process by studying critical events in tourism and politics that influence this process could be extremely valuable for shedding insights into how legitimation occurs. Process studies allow for more meaningful theorisation of the studied phenomenon because they take events and time "seriously" (Langley, 1999), given that change occurs over time and as a result of different events (Langley et al., 2013). Legitimation processes evolve, and different events, either at a certain point in time or over time, influence this process. Hence, we argue that it is important to employ "process thinking" when studying legitimation.

This book has also illustrated that the institutional environment is multifaceted, which makes it more challenging to analyse. Future studies that examine the institutional environment, should seek to undertake or at least acknowledge the importance of multi-level analysis and its implications for understanding organisational trajectories. Looking at different units of analysis together can provide a holistic picture of how institutions and various actors in the tourism industry co-evolve and operate and their effect on relationships between different stakeholders. These relationships are important, particularly in the context of developing economies, because they can dictate how effective or ineffective the enforcement mechanisms are.

Although different disciplines have different epistemological and ontological assumptions in the application of institutional theory, there is potential for the greater synthesis between different disciplines. Nevertheless, there is a need for a greater challenge to existing frameworks and assumptions, especially within more business-related disciplines that have tended to underplay the role of institutional analysis. For example, both the utilitarian and social/psychological approaches to change interventions noted in Table 4.2 are grounded in the ABC model. Social change is thought to depend upon values and attitudes (A), which are believed to drive the kinds of behaviour (B) that individuals choose (C) to adopt. The ABC model resonates with the current widely shared ideas about individual agency and media influence, but they underplay the role of structure and institutions. Explanations that give greater emphasis to structure "do not deny the possibility of meaningful policy action", seen in the ABC approach, "but at a minimum they recognise that effect is never in isolation and that interventions go on within, not outside, the processes they seek to shape" (Shove, 2010, p. 1278).

Conclusions: recognising our own institutions

As research on the history of the sciences has indicated, institutions play an extremely important role in determining the trajectories of research, given that they help establish the "rules of the game" (Hotimsky et al., 2006). Several reasons can be provided from an institutional perspective for the continued strength of the ABC approach. First, a successive series of governments in many developed countries have supported a research and tertiary education agenda that is increasingly focused on supposedly apolitical economic and market-oriented research deliverables (Demeritt, 2000) to which the ABC approach along with much contemporary economic and physical science analysis is a logical fit (Shove, 2010).

> This is not to deny that much reflective research has indeed taken place, but it is to suggest that much logical positivist science, with its apparent capacity to explain, solve and predict, but most of all serve those in power, has not surprisingly continued to find favour.
>
> (Unwin, 1992, p. 153)

Second,

> At a time when individuals, departments and institutions are increasingly being assessed in terms of the levels of grants that they attract, there is much pressure to obtain grants ... which frequently reflect the technical interest of logical positivism to maintain the social and political order.
>
> (Unwin, 1992, p. 153)

Third, the growth in the role of university and journal rankings as a means to not only measure the quality of research output but also influence academic hiring and rewards has favoured certain approaches, disciplines, and methods as well as problem definition over others. Fourth, the combination of the above has served to institutionalise particular approaches within universities and research institutions and structures as well as within government and organisational processes and systems. These issues reflect, particularly from the perspective of business and commercially oriented tourism and hospitality studies, a form of institutional "lock in" which makes policy and research learning and adaptation extremely difficult (Hall, 2011b).

Given that the ABC is the dominant paradigm in contemporary policymaking, "the scope of *relevant* social science is typically restricted to that which is theoretically consistent with it" (Shove, 2010, p. 1280, this author's emphasis). Policymakers fund and legitimise lines of enquiry that generate results that they can accept and manage, even if they do not necessarily provide a clear "solution" to a policy problem (Hall, 2014). The result is a self-fulfilling cycle of credibility (Latour & Woolgar, 1986), in which evidence of relevance and value to policymakers helps with securing additional resources for that approach. As Shove (2010) therefore opines, what does it take to get beyond the first three letters of the alphabet? Such an observation has implications for academic work as well as for policy problems and their solution. As Shove (2010) suggests, because of the current institutional constraints for research

> paradigms and approaches which lie beyond the pale of the ABC are doomed to be forever marginal no matter how interactive or how policy-engaged their advocates might be. To break through this log jam it would be necessary to reopen a set of basic questions about the role of the state, the allocation of responsibility, and in very practical terms the meaning of manageability.
>
> (Shove, 2010, p. 1283)

The dominant material positivist ontology of natural science and its adoption in some areas of the social sciences, especially in economics, marketing, management, and much of tourism and hospitality is, to many people, the discourse of "normal science" because of the perceived authority of its empiricist and quantitative form, but it is also a position that often engenders mistrust and is open to critique. As Demeritt (2001, p. 309) suggests in the context of climate change research, instead of denying the socially situated and contingent nature of scientific knowledge, there is a need "to develop a more reflexive understanding of science as a situated and ongoing social practice" (see also Mann, 2016 on reflexive research practices).

Demeritt's (2001) observation is a further reinforcement of Feyerabend's (1993) critique of science:

> The success of "science" cannot be used as an argument for treating as yet unsolved problems in a standardized way ... "non-scientific" procedures cannot be pushed aside by argument ... the public can participate in the discussion without disturbing existing roads to success ... in cases where the scientists' work affects the public it even should participate ... a full democratisation of science (which includes the protection of minorities such as scientists) is not in conflict with science. It is in conflict with a philosophy, often called "Rationalism", that uses a frozen image of science to terrorize people unfamiliar with its practice ... there can be many different kinds of science.
>
> (Feyerabend, 1993, p. 2)

Institutions are fundamental to tourism and hospitality, and it is therefore not surprising that there is a rapid expansion of interest in and application of institutional theory. However, it is vital that institutions and their analysis are recognised as essentially contested concepts (Gallie, 1955/56), the definition and application of which is inherently a matter of dispute as definition pre-determines the concept's application: "concepts the proper use of which inevitably involves endless disputes about their proper uses on the part of their user" (Gallie, 1955/56, p. 169). This means that in the study of institutions there is also a range of ontologies that frame different worldviews and methods and which, sometimes unknowingly to their holders, favour certain interests and forms of knowledge. If a truly integrated approach to institutions and the institutional environment is to be achieved in tourism and hospitality in order to better understand organisations, policies, stakeholders, and the role of the state, it therefore becomes vital to realise that there needs to be greater transparency and respect of the value of different knowledges, approaches, and methods as well as an appreciation of the advantages and disadvantages of different ontological positions. Institutions set the rules of the game. In terms of the study of institutions it is appropriate that the rules of the game are kept as wide and as transparent as possible.

References

Adam, C., Bauer, M. W., Knill, C., & Studinger, P. (2007). The termination of public organizations: Theoretical perspectives to revitalize a promising research area. *Public Organization Review*, *7*(3), 221–236.

Adie, B., Amore, A., & Hall, C. M. (2020). Just because it seems impossible, doesn't mean we shouldn't at least try: The need for longitudinal perspectives on tourism partnerships and the SDGs. *Journal of Sustainable Tourism*. doi: 10.1080/09669582.2020.1860071

Ahlstrom, D., Bruton, G. D., & Yeh, K. S. (2008). Private firms in China: Building legitimacy in an emerging economy. *Journal of World Business*, *43*(4), 385–399.

Ahmadjian, C. L. (2016). Comparative institutional analysis and institutional complexity. *Journal of Management Studies*, *53*(1), 12–27.

Ahmadjian, C. L., & Robinson, P. (2001). Safety in numbers: Downsizing and the deinstitutionalization of permanent employment in Japan. *Administrative Science Quarterly*, *46*(4), 622–654.

Aldrich, H. E., & Fiol, C. M. (1994). Fools rush in? The institutional context of industry creation. *Academy of Management Journal*, *19*(4), 645–670.

Alexander, E. A. (2012). The effects of legal, normative, and cultural–cognitive institutions on innovation in technology alliances. *Management International Review*, *52*(6), 791–815.

Allee, T. L., & Huth, P. K. (2006). Legitimizing dispute settlement: International legal rulings as domestic political cover. *American Political Science Review*, *100*(2), 219–234.

Almandoz, J. (2014). Founding teams as carriers of competing logics: When institutional forces predict banks' risk exposure. *Administrative Science Quarterly*, *59*(3), 442–473.

Amore, A., & Hall, C. M. (2016). From governance to meta-governance in tourism? Re-incorporating politics, interests and values in the analysis of tourism governance. *Tourism Recreation Research*, *41*(2), 109–122.

Amore, A., & Hall, C. M. (2017). National and urban public policy in tourism. Towards the emergence of a hyperneoliberal script? *International Journal of Tourism Policy*, *7*(1), 4–22.

Armanios, F., & Ergene, B. A. (2018). *Halal food: A history.* Oxford University Press.

Arndt, J. (1981). The political economy of marketing systems: Reviving the institutional approach. *Journal of Macromarketing, 1*(2), 36–47.

Aureli, S., Medei, R., Supino, E., & Travaglini, C. (2017). Sustainability disclosure and a legitimacy crisis: Insights from two major cruise companies. *European Journal of Tourism Research, 17,* 149–163.

Azari, J. R., & Smith, J. K. (2012). Unwritten rules: Informal institutions in established democracies. *Perspectives on Politics, 10*(1), 37–55.

Baird, T., Hall, C. M., & Castka, P. (2018). New Zealand winegrowers attitudes and behaviours towards wine tourism and sustainable winegrowing. *Sustainability, 10*(3), 797.

Bansal, P., & Roth, K. (2000). Why companies go green: A model of ecological responsiveness. *Academy of Management Journal, 43*(4), 717–736.

Baranov, A., Malkov, E., Polishchuk, L., Rochlitz, M., & Syunyaev, G. (2015). How (not) to measure Russian regional institutions. *Russian Journal of Economics, 1*(2), 154–181.

Barnett, M. (1990). High politics is low politics: The domestic and systemic sources of Israeli security policy, 1967–1977. *World Politics, 42*(04), 529–562.

Bartley, T., & Zhang, L. (2012). *Opening the "black box": Transnational private certification of labor standards in China.* RCCPB Working Paper No. 18. Research Center for Chinese Politics and Business, Indiana University.

Beetham, D. (1991). *The legitimation of power.* MacMillan.

Beetham, D. (1993). In defence of legitimacy. Debate. *Political Studies, 41*(3), 488–491.

Beeton, S. (2005). The case study in tourism research: A multi-method case study approach. In B. W. Ritchie, C. A. Palmer, & P. M. Burns (Eds.), *Tourism research methods: Integrating theory with practice* (pp. 37–48). CABI.

Berger, P. L., & Luckmann, T. (1967). *The social construction of reality: A treatise in the sociology of knowledge.* Anchor.

Bertels, S., & Lawrence, T. B. (2016). Organisational responses to institutional complexity stemming from emerging logics: The role of individuals. *Strategic Organization, 14*(4), 336–372.

Besharov, M. L., & Smith, W. K. (2014). Multiple institutional logics in organizations: Explaining their varied nature and implications. *Academy of Management Review, 39*(3), 364–381.

Biber, E., Light, S. E., Ruhl, J. B., & Salzman, J. (2017). Regulating business innovation as policy disruption: From the Model T to Airbnb. *Vanderbilt Law Review, 70,* 1561–1626.

Bitektine, A. (2011). Toward a theory of social judgments of organisations: The case of legitimacy, reputation, and status. *Academy of Management Review, 36*(1), 151–179.

Bitektine, A., & Haack, P. (2015). The "macro" and the "micro" of legitimacy: Toward a multilevel theory of the legitimacy process. *Academy of Management Review, 40*(1), 49–75.

Black, B. S., & Tarassova, A. S. (2003). Institutional reform in transition: A case study of Russia. *Supreme Court Economic Review*, *10*, 211–278.

Boddewyn, J., & Brewer, T. (1994). International business political behaviour: New theoretical directions. *Academy of Management Review*, *19*(1), 119–143.

Boddewyn, J. J. (2016). International business–government relations research 1945–2015: Concepts, typologies, theories and methodologies. *Journal of World Business*, *51*(1), 10–22.

Boin, A., Kuipers, S., & Steenbergen, M. (2010). The life and death of public organizations: A question of institutional design? *Governance*, *23*(3), 385–410.

Boone, C., & Özcan, S. (2020). Oppositional logics and the antecedents of hybridization: A country-level study of the diffusion of Islamic banking windows, 1975–2017. *Organization Science*. doi: 10.1287/orsc.2019.1338

Bramwell, B., & Lane, B. (Eds.). (2000a). *Tourism collaboration and partnerships: Politics, practice and sustainability*. Channelview.

Bramwell, B., & Lane, B. (2000b). Collaboration and partnerships in tourism planning. In B. Bramwell & B. Lane (Eds.), *Tourism collaboration and partnerships: Politics, practice and sustainability* (pp. 1–19). Channelview.

Brinks, D. M. (2003). Informal institutions and the rule of law: The judicial response to state killings in Buenos Aires and São Paulo in the 1990s. *Comparative Politics*, *26*(1), 1–19.

Bromley, P., & Powell, W. W. (2012). From smoke and mirrors to walking the talk: Decoupling in the contemporary world. *Academy of Management Annals*, *6*(1), 483–530.

Buchanan, J. M., & Tullock, G. (1962). *The calculus of consent: Logical foundations of constitutional democracy*. University of Michigan Press.

Campbell, D. (1975). "Degree of freedom" and the case study. *Comparative Political Studies*, *8*(2), 178–193.

Carpenter, D., & Lewis, D. E. (2004). Political learning from rare events: Poisson inference, fiscal constraints, and the lifetime of bureaus. *Political Analysis*, *12*(3), 201–232.

Carrillo-Hidalgo, I., & Pulido-Fernández, J. I. (2019). The role of the World Bank in the inclusive financing of tourism as an instrument of sustainable development. *Sustainability*, *12*(1), 1–21.

Casanueva, C., Gallego, Á., & García-Sánchez, M. R. (2016). Social network analysis in tourism. *Current Issues in Tourism*, *19*(12), 1190–1209.

Causevic, S., & Lynch, P. (2013). Political (in) stability and its influence on tourism development. *Tourism Management*, *34*, 145–157.

Caussat, P., Prime, N., & Wilken, R. (2019). How multinational banks in India gain legitimacy: Organisational practices and resources required for implementation. *Management International Review*, *59*(4), 561–591.

Chen, G., Huang, S., & Bao, J. (2016). The multiple logics of tourism development in China. *Journal of Sustainable Tourism*, *24*(12), 1655–1673.

Cheung, Z., Aalto, E., & Nevalainen, P. (2020). Institutional logics and the internationalization of a state-owned enterprise: Evaluation of international venture opportunities by Telecom Finland 1987–1998. *Journal of World Business*, *55*(6). doi: 10.1016/j.jwb.2020.101140

Child, J., & Tsai, T. (2005). The dynamic between firms' environmental strategies and institutional constraints in emerging economies: Evidence from China and Taiwan. *Journal of Management Studies*, *42*(1), 95–125.

Coase, R. (1937). The nature of the firm. *Economica*, *4*(16), 386–405.

Coase, R. (1998). The new institutional economics. *The American Economic Review*, *88*(2), 72–74.

Coles, T., & Hall, C. M. (Eds.). (2008). *International business and tourism: Global issues, contemporary interactions*. Routledge.

Collier, D., Laporte. J., & Seawright, D. (2008). Typologies: Forming concepts and creating categorical variables. In J. M. Box-Steffensmeier, H. E. Brady, & D. Collier (Eds.), *The Oxford handbook of political methodology* (pp. 152–173). Oxford University Press.

Commons, J. R. (1924). *Legal foundations of capitalism*. Transaction Publishing.

Cordano, M., & Frieze, I. H. (2000). Pollution reduction preferences of US environmental managers: Applying Ajzen's theory of planned behaviour. *Academy of Management Journal*, *43*(4), 627–641.

Creed, W. D., DeJordy, R., & Lok, J. (2010). Being the change: Resolving institutional contradiction through identity work. *Academy of Management Journal*, *53*(6), 1336–1364.

Crook, R. C. (1987). Legitimacy, authority and the transfer of power in Ghana. *Political Studies*, *35*(4), 552–572.

Cudworth, E., Hall, T., & McGovern, J. (2007). *The modern state: Theories and ideologies*. Edinburgh University Press.

Cuervo-Cazurra, A., Inkpen, A., Musacchio, A., & Ramaswamy, K. (2014). Governments as owners: State-owned multinational companies. *Journal of International Business Studies*, *45*(8), 919–942.

Czernek, K. (2017). Tourism features as determinants of knowledge transfer in the process of tourist cooperation. *Current Issues in Tourism*, *20*(2), 204–220.

D'Aunno, T., Succi, M., & Alexander, A. (2000). The role of institutional and market forces in divergent organisational change. *Administrative Science Quarterly*, *45*(4), 679–703.

Dacin, M. T, Goodstein, J., & Scott, W. R. (2002). Theory and institutional change: Introduction to the special research forum. *Academy of Management Journal*, *45*(1), 43–56.

Damaska, M. R. (1986). *The faces of justice and state authority: A comparative approach to the legal process*. Yale University Press.

Dang, Q. T., Jasovska, P., & Rammal, H. G. (2020). International business-government relations: The risk management strategies of MNEs in emerging economies. *Journal of World Business*, *55*(1), 101042.

Darbi, W. P. K., & Hall, C. M. (2014). Elite interviews: Critical practice and tourism. *Current Issues in Tourism*, *17*(9), 832–848.

Dashwood, H. S. (2012). CSR norms and organizational learning in the mining sector. *Corporate Governance*, *12*(1), 118–138.

Dashwood, H. S. (2014). Sustainable development and industry self-regulation: Developments in the global mining sector. *Business & Society, 53*(4), 551–582.

Dau, L. A. (2016). Knowledge will set you free. Enhancing the firm's responsiveness to institutional change. *International Journal of Emerging Markets, 11*(2), 121–147.

De Crespigny, A. R. C., & McKinnel, R. T. (1960). The nature and significance of economic boycott. *South African Journal of Economics, 28*(4), 319–336.

De Grosbois, D. (2016). Corporate social responsibility reporting in the cruise tourism industry: A performance evaluation using a new institutional theory based model. *Journal of Sustainable Tourism, 24*(2), 245–269.

De Urioste-Stone, S., McLaughlin, W. J., Daigle, J. J., & Fefer, J. P. (2018). Applying case study methodology to tourism research. In R. Nunkoo (Ed.), *Handbook of research methods for tourism and hospitality management* (pp. 407–427). Edward Elgar.

DeBoer, J., Panwar, R., & Rivera, J. (2017). Toward a place-based understanding of business sustainability: The role of green competitors and green locales in firms' voluntary environmental engagement. *Business Strategy & the Environment, 26*(7), 940–955.

Deephouse, D. L. (1996). Does isomorphism legitimate? *Academy of Management Journal, 39*(4), 1024–1039.

Deephouse, D. L., & Carter, S. M. (2005). An examination of differences between organisational legitimacy and organisational reputation. *Journal of Management Studies, 42*(2), 329–360.

Deephouse, D. L., Bundy, J., Tost, L. P., & Suchman, M. C. (2017). Organisational legitimacy: Six key questions. In R. Greenwood, C. Oliver, T. Lawrence, & R. Meyer (Eds.), *The SAGE handbook of organisational institutionalism* (pp. 27–54.). SAGE.

Dela Santa, E. (2013). The politics of implementing Philippine tourism policy: A policy network and advocacy coalition framework approach. *Asia Pacific Journal of Tourism Research, 18*(8), 913–933.

Delacote, P. (2009). On the sources of consumer boycotts ineffectiveness. *The Journal of Environment & Development, 18*(3), 306–322.

Deleuze, G. (1994). *Difference and repetition.* Columbia University Press.

Delios, A. (2010). How can organisations be competitive but dare to care? *Academy of Management Perspectives, 24*(3), 25–36.

Delmas, M. A., & Toffel, W. M. (2008). Organizational responses to environmental demands: Opening the black box. *Strategic Management Journal, 29*(10), 1027–1055.

Demeritt, D. (2000). The new social contract for Science: Accountability, relevance, and value in US and UK science and research policy. *Antipode, 32*(3), 308–329.

Demeritt, D. (2001). The construction of global warming and the politics of science. *Annals of the Association of American Geographers, 91*(2), 307–337.

Denzin, N. K. (1989). *The research act* (3rd ed.). Prentice Hall.

Desai, V. M. (2016). Under the radar: Regulatory collaborations and their selective use to facilitate organisational compliance. *Academy of Management Journal, 59*(2), 636–657.

Dewey, J. (1938). *Experience and education.* Collier Books.

Dicen, K. B., Yodsuwan, C., Butcher, K., & Mingkwan, N. (2019). The institutional context for experiential learning investment in hospitality education: A case study from Thailand. In C. Liu & H. Schänzel (Eds.), *Tourism education and Asia. Perspectives on Asian tourism* (pp. 143–160). Springer.

Díez-Martín, F., Prado-Roman, C., & Blanco-González, A. (2013). Beyond legitimacy: Legitimacy types and organisational success. *Management Decision, 51*(10), 1954–1969.

DiMaggio, P. J., & Powell, W. W. (1983). The iron cage revisited: Institutional isomorphism and collective rationality in organisational fields. *American Sociological Review, 48*(2), 147–160.

DiMaggio, P. J., & Powell, W. W. (1991). Introduction. In W. W. Powell & P. J. DiMaggio (Eds.), *The new institutionalism in organizational analysis* (pp. 1–38). University of Chicago Press.

Dodds, R. (2007). Sustainable tourism and policy implementation: Lessons from the case of Calvia, Spain. *Current Issues in Tourism, 10*(4), 296–322.

Dogan, M., & Pelassy, D. (1990). *How to compare nations. Strategies in comparative politics* (2nd ed.). Chatham House.

Dowling, J., & Pfeffer, J. (1975). Organisational legitimacy: Social values and organisational behavior. *Pacific Sociological Review,* 18(1), 22–136.

Drori, I., & Honig, B. (2013). A process model of internal and external legitimacy. *Organization Studies, 34*(3), 345–376.

Earl, A. (2021). Methodological issues in examining sanctions: Reflection on conducting research in Russia. *Tourism Management Perspectives,* in press.

Easton, D. (1965). *A systems analysis of political life.* Wiley.

Egri, C., & Herman, S. (2000). Leadership in the North American environmental sector: Values, leadership styles and contexts of environmental leaders and their organizations. *Academy of Management Journal, 43*(4), 44–63.

Eisenhardt, K. M. (1989). Building theories from case study research. *Academy of Management Review, 14*(4), 532–550.

Elsahn, Z., Callagher, L., Husted, K., Korber, S., & Siedlok, F. (2020). Are rigor and transparency enough? Review and future directions for case studies in technology and innovation Management. *R&D Management, 50*(3), 309–328.

Elsbach, K. D., & Sutton, R. I. (1992). Acquiring organisational legitimacy through illegitimate actions: A marriage of institutional and impression management theories. *Academy of Management Journal, 35*(4), 699–738.

Elster, J. (1986). The market and the forum. In J. Elster & A. Hylland (Eds.), *Foundations of social choice theory* (pp. 106–107). Cambridge University Press.

Engel, U., Gebauer, C., & Hüncke, A. (Eds.). (2015). *Notes from within and without – research permits between requirements and "realities".* Working Papers of the Priority Programme 1448 of the German Research Foundation No. 16. University of Halle.

Esteban-Lloret, N. N., Aragón-Sánchez, A., & Carrasco-Hernández, A. (2018). Determinants of employee training: Impact on organizational legitimacy and organizational performance. *The International Journal of Human Resource Management, 29*(6), 1208–1229.

Evans, P. (1995). *Embedded autonomy: States and industrials transformation.* Princeton University Press.

Evans, P., Ryeschemeyer, D., & Skocpol, T. (1985). *Bringing the state back in.* Cambridge University Press.

Fadda, S. (2012). *Formal and informal institutions: Towards a deeper understanding of a complex relationship. Some cases in the labour market.* Working Paper, No. 02. ASTRIL.

Farah, M. F., & Newman, A. J. (2010). Exploring consumer boycott intelligence using a socio-cognitive approach. *Journal of Business Research, 63*(4), 347–355.

Farmaki, A., Altinay, L., Botterill, D., & Hilke, S. (2015). Politics and sustainable tourism: The case of Cyprus. *Tourism Management, 47*, 178–190.

Faulconbridge, J., & Muzio, D. (2016). Global professional service firms and the challenge of institutional complexity: "Field relocation" as a response strategy. *Journal of Management Studies, 53*(1), 89–124.

Feyerabend, P. (1993). *Against method* (3rd ed.). Verso.

Flick, U. (1992). Triangulation revisited: Strategy of validation or alternative? *Journal for the Theory of Social Behaviour, 22*(2), 175–198.

Fong, V. H. I., Wong, I. A., & Hong, J. F. L. (2018). Developing institutional logics in the tourism industry through coopetition. *Tourism Management, 66*, 244–262.

Font, X., Bonilla-Priego, M. J., & Kantenbacher, J. (2019). Trade associations as corporate social responsibility actors: An institutional theory analysis of animal welfare in tourism. *Journal of Sustainable Tourism, 27*(1), 118–138.

Fontana, A., & Frey, J. H. (2005). The interview: From neutral stance to political involvement. In N. K. Denzin & Y. S. Lincoln (Eds.), *The Sage handbook of qualitative research* (pp. 695–727). SAGE.

Food and Agriculture Organization of the United Nations (FAO) & World Health Organization (WHO). (2001). General guidelines for use of the term "Halal" CAC/GL 24-1997. In Codex Alimentarius (Revised). FAO. http://www.fao.org /3/Y2770E/y2770e08.htm

Forstenlechner, I., & Mellahi, K. (2011). Gaining legitimacy through hiring local workforce at a premium: The case of MNEs in the United Arab Emirates. *Journal of World Business, 46*(4), 455–461.

Gallie, W. B. (1955/6). Essentially contested concepts. *Proceedings of the Aristotelian Society, 56*, 167–198.

Garrone, P., Piscitello, L., & D'Amelio, M. (2019). Multinational enterprises and the provision of collective goods in developing countries under formal and informal institutional voids. The case of electricity in sub-Saharan Africa. *Journal of International Management, 25*(2), 100650.

Gel'man, V. (2015). *Authoritarian Russia: Analyzing post-soviet regime changes.* University of Pittsburgh Press.

Gel'man, V., & Ryzhenkov, S. (2011). Local regimes, sub-national governance and the "power vertical" in contemporary Russia. *Europe-Asia Studies*, *63*(3), 449–465.

Gelles, R. J. (1974). The television news interview: A field study. *Journal of Applied Communication Research*, *2*(1), 31–44.

Giddens, A. (1994). *The constitution of society*. Polity Press.

Gilison, J. M. (1967). New factors of stability in Soviet collective leadership. *World Politics: A Quarterly Journal of International Relations*, *19*(4), 563–581.

Gillen, J. (2011). Off the record: Segmenting informal discussion into viable methodological categories. In C. M. Hall (Ed.), *Fieldwork in tourism: Methods, issues and reflections* (pp. 199–208). Routledge.

Gilley, B. (2006). The meaning and measure of state legitimacy: Results for 72 countries. *European Journal of Political Research*, *45*(3), 499–525.

Glaser, B. G. (1992). *Basics of grounded theory analysis*. Sociological Press.

Gölgeci, I., Assadinia, S., Kuivalainen, O., & Larimo, J. (2019). Emerging-market firms' dynamic capabilities and international performance: The moderating role of institutional development and distance. *International Business Review*, *28*(6). doi: 10.1016/j.ibusrev.2019.101593

Gorynia, M., Nowak, J., Trąpczyński, P., & Wolniak, R. (2019). Friend or foe? On the role of institutional reforms in the investment development path of Central and East European economies. *International Business Review*, *28*(3), 575–587.

Gössling, S., & Buckley, R. (2016). Carbon labels in tourism: Persuasive communication? *Journal of Cleaner Production*, *111*, 358–369.

Gössling, S., Hall, C. M., & Andersson, A. C. (2018). The manager's dilemma: A conceptualization of online review manipulation strategies. *Current Issues in Tourism*, *21*(5), 484–503.

Gössling, S., Zeiss, H., Hall, C. M., Martin-Rios, C., Ram, Y., & Grøtte, I. P. (2019). A cross-country comparison of accommodation manager perspectives on online review manipulation. *Current Issues in Tourism*, *22*(14), 1744–1763.

Greenwood, R., Raynard, M., Kodeih, F., Micelotta, E. R., & Lounsbury, M. (2011). Institutional complexity and organisational responses. *Academy of Management Annals*, *5*(1), 317–371.

Greenwood, R., Suddaby, R., & Hinings, C. R. (2002). Theorizing change: The role of professional associations in the transformation of institutionalized fields. *Academy of Management Journal*, *45*(1), 58–80.

Gretzel, U., Mendes-Filho, L., Lobianco, M., Vazquez, M. A., & Mistilis, N. (2017). Technology adoption by tourism operators in Australia and Brazil: An institutional theory perspective. *e-Review of Tourism Research*, *8*, 1–5. https://ag rilifecdn.tamu.edu/ertr/files/2016/12/RN180.pdf

Grewal, R., & Dharwadkar, R. (2002). The role of the institutional environment in marketing channels. *Journal of Marketing*, *66*(3), 82–97.

Grzymala-Busse, A. (2010). The best laid plans: The impact of informal rules on formal institutions in transition regimes. *Studies in Comparative International Development*, *45*(3), 311–333.

Guix, M., Bonilla-Priego, M. J., & Font, X. (2018). The process of sustainability reporting in international hotel groups: An analysis of stakeholder inclusiveness, materiality and responsiveness. *Journal of Sustainable Tourism, 26*(7), 1063–1084.

Gümüsay, A. A., Smets, M., & Morris, T. (2020). "God at work": Engaging central and incompatible institutional logics through elastic hybridity. *Academy of Management Journal, 63*(1), 124–154.

Gyau, A., & Stringer, R. (2011). Institutional isomorphism and adoption of e-marketing in the hospitality industry: A new perspective for research. In K. Sidali, A. Spiller, & B. Schulze (Eds.), *Food, agri-culture and tourism* (pp. 130–139). Springer.

Hall, C. M. (1999). Rethinking collaboration and partnership: A public policy perspective. *Journal of Sustainable Tourism, 7*(3–4), 274–289.

Hall, C. M. (2008). *Tourism planning* (2nd ed.). Pearson.

Hall, C. M. (2009). Archetypal approaches to implementation and their implications for tourism policy. *Tourism Recreation Research, 34*(3), 235–245.

Hall, C. M. (2010a). Politics and tourism – interdependency and implications in understanding change. In R. Butler & W. Suntikul (Eds.), *Tourism and political change* (pp. 7–18). Goodfellow Publishers.

Hall, C. M. (2010b). Tourism and the implementation of the Convention on Biological Diversity. *Journal of Heritage Tourism, 5*(4), 267–284.

Hall, C. M. (2011a). A typology of governance and its implications for tourism policy analysis. *Journal of Sustainable Tourism, 19*(4–5), 437–457.

Hall, C. M. (2011b). Policy learning and policy failure in sustainable tourism governance: From first-and second-order to third-order change? *Journal of Sustainable Tourism, 19*(4–5), 649–671.

Hall, C. M. (Ed.). (2011c). *Fieldwork in tourism: Methods, issues reflections.* Routledge.

Hall, C. M. (2011d). Researching the political in tourism: Where knowledge meets power. In C. M. Hall (Ed.), *Fieldwork in tourism: Methods, issues and reflections* (pp. 39–54). Routledge.

Hall, C. M. (2011e). Concluding thoughts: Where does fieldwork end and tourism begin? In C. M. Hall (Ed.), *Fieldwork in tourism: Methods, issues and reflections* (pp. 315–318). Routledge.

Hall, C. M. (2011f). Fieldwork in tourism/touring fields: Where does tourism end and fieldwork begin? In C. M. Hall (Ed.), *Fieldwork in tourism: Methods, issues and reflections* (pp. 7–18). Routledge.

Hall, C. M. (2014). *Tourism and social marketing.* Routledge.

Hall, C. M. (2016a). Putting ecological thinking back in to disaster ecology and responses to natural disasters: Rethinking resilience or business as usual? In C. M. Hall, S. Malinen, R. Vosslamber & R. Wordsworth (Eds.), *Post-disaster management: Business, organisational and consumer resilience and the Christchurch earthquakes* (pp. 269–292). Routledge.

Hall, C. M. (2016b). Intervening in academic interventions: Framing social marketing's potential for successful sustainable tourism behavioural change. *Journal of Sustainable Tourism, 24*(3), 350–375.

Hall, C. M., & Jenkins, J. M. (1995). *Tourism and public policy.* Routledge.

Hall, C. M., & Page, S. J. (2014). *Geography of tourism and recreation*. Routledge.

Hall, C. M., & Prayag, G. (Eds.). (2020). *The Routledge handbook of halal hospitality and Islamic tourism*. Routledge.

Hall, C. M., Prayag, G., & Amore, A. (2017). *Tourism and resilience: Individual, organisational and destination perspectives*. Channel View.

Hall, C. M., & Rusher, K. (2004). Risky lifestyles? Entrepreneurial characteristics of the New Zealand bed and breakfast sector. In R. Thomas (Ed.), *Small firms in tourism: International perspectives* (pp. 83–97). Elsevier.

Hall, C. M., & Veer, E. (2016). The DMO is dead. Long live the DMO (or, why DMO managers don't care about post-structuralism). *Tourism Recreation Research*, *41*(3), 354–357.

Hall, C. M., & Williams, A. M. (2020). *Tourism and innovation* (2nd ed.). Routledge.

Hall, C. M., Dayal, N., Majstorovic, D., Mills, H., Paul-Andrews, L., Wallace, C., & Truong, V. D. (2016). Accommodation consumers and providers' attitudes, behaviours and practices for sustainability: A systematic review. *Sustainability*, *8*(7), 625.

Hall, P. A., & Taylor, R. C. R. (1996). Political science and the three new institutionalisms, *Political Studies*, *44*(5), 936–957.

Hardy, A. (2005). Using grounded theory to explore stakeholder perceptions of tourism. *Journal of Tourism and Cultural Change*, *3*(2), 108–133.

Haseeb, M., & Azam, M. (2020). Dynamic nexus among tourism, corruption, democracy and environmental degradation: A panel data investigation. *Environment, Development and Sustainability*. doi: 10.1007/s10668-020-00832-9

Hassan, A., Kennell, J., & Chaperon, S. (2020). Rhetoric and reality in Bangladesh: Elite stakeholder perceptions of the implementation of tourism policy. *Tourism Recreation Research*, *45*(3), 307–322.

Helmke, G., & Levitsky, S. (2004). Informal institutions and comparative politics: A research agenda. *Perspectives on Politics*, *2*(4), 725–740.

Hernes, T. (2014). *A process theory of organization*. Oxford University Press.

Herold, D. M., & Lee, K. H. (2019). The influence of internal and external pressures on carbon management practices and disclosure strategies. *Australasian Journal of Environmental Management*, *26*(1), 63–81.

Hirsch, P. M., & Lounsbury, M. (1997). Putting the organization back into organization theory: Action, change, and the "new" institutionalism. *Journal of Management Inquiry*, *6*(1), 79–88.

Hirsch, P. M., & Lounsbury, M. (2015). Toward a more critical and "powerful" institutionalism. *Journal of Management Inquiry*, *24*(1), 96–99.

Hoffman, A. J. (1999). Institutional evolution and change: Environmentalism and the US chemical industry. *Academy of Management Journal*, *42*(4), 351–371.

Hoffman, A. J. (2001). Linking organizational and field-level analyses – The diffusion of corporate environmental practice. *Organization and Environment*, *14*(2), 133–156.

Hotimsky, S., Cobb, R., & Bond, A. (2006). Contracts or scripts? A critical review of the application of institutional theories to the study of environmental change.

Ecology and Society, 11(1), 41. http://www.ecologyandsociety.org/vol11/iss1/a rt41/

Huang-Horowitz, N. C., & Evans, S. K. (2020). Communicating organizational identity as part of the legitimation process: A case study of small firms in an emerging field. *International Journal of Business Communication, 57*(3), 327–351.

Hughes, E., & Scheyvens, R. (2016). Corporate social responsibility in tourism post-2015: A development first approach. *Tourism Geographies, 18*(5), 469–482.

Immergut, E. M. (1998). The theoretical core of the new institutionalism. *Politics & Society, 26*(1), 5–34.

Immergut, E. M. (2006). Historical-institutionalism in political science and the problem of change. In A. Wimmer & R. Kössler (Eds.), *Understanding change: Models, methodologies, and metaphors* (pp. 237–259). Palgrave Macmillan.

Ingstrup, M. B., Aarikka-Stenroos, L., & Adlin, N. (2020). When institutional logics meet: Alignment and misalignment in collaboration between academia and practitioners. *Industrial Marketing Management*. doi: 10.1016/j. indmarman.2020.01.004.

Jamali, D. (2010). MNCs and international accountability standards through an institutional lens: Evidence of symbolic conformity or decoupling. *Journal of Business Ethics, 95*, 617–640.

Jansson, H., Johanson, M., & Ramström, J. (2007). Institutions and business networks: A comparative analysis of the Chinese, Russian, and West European markets. *Industrial Marketing Management, 36*(7), 955–967.

Jessop, B. (1997). Capitalism and its future: Remarks on regulation, government and governance. *Review of International Political Economy, 4*(3), 561–581.

Jessop, B. (2011). Metagovernance. In M. Bevir (Ed.), *The SAGE handbook of governance* (pp. 106–123). SAGE.

Jick, T. D. (1979). Mixing qualitative and quantitative methods: Triangulation in action. *Administrative Science Quarterly, 24*(4), 602–611.

Johansen, C. B., & Waldorff, S. B. (2015). *What are institutional logics?* [Paper presentation]. Academy of Management Annual Meeting 2015, Vancouver, Canada.

Johansson, L. (2015). Dangerous liaisons: Risk, positionality and power in women's anthropological fieldwork. *Journal of the Anthropological Society of Oxford, 7*(1), 55–63.

Josephs, L. (2019). Lawmakers slam FAA over handling of Boeing 737 Max. *CNBC*, 31 July. https://www.cnbc.com/2019/07/31/faa-officials-face-senate-ov er-boeing-737-max-crashes.html

Judge, D., Stoker, G., & Wolman, H. (1995). Urban politics and theory: An introduction. In D. Judge, G. Stoker & H. Wolman (Eds.), *Theories of urban politics* (pp. 1–12). SAGE.

Karhunen, P. (2008). Toward convergence in the St. Petersburg hotel industry through the lens of institutional theory. *Journal for East European Management Studies, 13*(2), 106–128.

Kaufman, H. (1976). *Are government organizations immortal?* Brookings Institution.

Kauppi, K. (2013). Extending the use of institutional theory in operations and supply chain management research. *International Journal of Operations & Production Management*, *33*(10), 1318–1345.

Kay, A. (2006). *The dynamics of public policy: Theory and evidence*. Edward Elgar.

Khanna, T., & Palepu, K. (2005). The evolution of concentrated ownership in India: broad patterns and a history of the Indian software industry. In R. K. Morck (Ed.), *A history of corporate governance around the world: Family business groups to professional managers* (pp. 283–324). University of Chicago Press.

Kitschelt, H. (2000). Linkages between citizens and politicians in democratic politics. *Comparative Political Studies*, *33*(6–7), 845–879.

Kloß, S. T. (2017). Sexual(ized) harassment and ethnographic fieldwork: A silenced aspect of social research. *Ethnography*, *18*(3), 396–414.

Köllner, P. (2013). *Informal institutions in autocracies: Analytical perspectives and the case of the Chinese Communist Party*. Working Paper 232. GIGA.

Kooiman, J. (2003). *Governing as governance*. SAGE.

Kooiman, J., & Jentoft, S. (2009). Meta-governance: Values, norms and principles, and the making of hard choices. *Public Administration*, *87*(4), 818–836.

Kornilaki, M., & Font, X. (2019). Normative influences: How socio-cultural and industrial norms influence the adoption of sustainability practices. A grounded theory of Cretan, small tourism firms. *Journal of Environmental Management*, *230*, 183–189.

Kostova, T., & Roth, K. (2002). Adoption of an organisational practice by subsidiaries of multinational corporations: Institutional and relational effects. *Academy of Management Journal*, *45*(1), 215–233.

Kostova, T., & Zaheer, S. (1999). Organisational legitimacy under conditions of complexity: The case of the multinational enterprise. *Academy of Management Review*, *24*(1), 64–81.

Kostova, T., Roth, K., & Dacin, T. (2008). Institutional theory in the study of multinational corporations: A critique and new directions. *Academy of Management Review*, *33*(4), 994–1007.

Kovats-Bernat, J. C. (2002). Negotiating dangerous fields: Pragmatic strategies for fieldwork amid violence and terror. *American Anthropologist*, *104*(1), 208–222.

Kraatz, M. S., & Block, E. S. (2008). Organisational implications of institutional pluralism. In R. Greenwood, C. Oliver, R. Suddaby & K. Sahil-Andersson (Eds.), *The SAGE handbook of organisational institutionalism* (pp. 243–275). SAGE.

Kujala, J., Battista, V., Lucianetti, L., & Paavilainen, A. (2020). The influence of cultural context in managerial decision-making: Legitimacy views of Finnish and Italian managers. *International Journal of Human Resources Development and Management* [pdf]. https://www.researchgate.net/profile/Johanna_Kujal a/publication/345629460_The_influence_of_cultural_context_in_manageria l_decision-making_legitimacy_views_of_Finnish_and_Italian_managers/links /5fa96187458515157bf7455b/The-influence-of-cultural-context-in-managerial -decision-making-legitimacy-views-of-Finnish-and-Italian-managers.pdf

Labonté, R., Crooks, V. A., Valdés, A. C., Runnels, V., & Snyder, J. (2018). Government roles in regulating medical tourism: Evidence from Guatemala. *International Journal for Equity in Health, 17*(150). doi: 10.1186/s12939-018-0866-1

Lakatos, I. (1971). History of science and its rational reconstruction. In R. Buck & R. Cohen (Eds.), *PSA 1970. In memory of Rudolf Carnap. Proceedings of the 1970 biennial meeting Philosophy of Science Association.* Boston Studies in the Philosophy of Science, Vol. 8 (pp. 92–122). Reidel.

Langley, A. (1999). Strategies for theorizing from process data. *Academy of Management Review, 24*(4), 691–710.

Langley, A. N. N., Smallman, C., Tsoukas, H., & Van de Ven, A. H. (2013). Process studies of change in organisation and management: Unveiling temporality, activity, and flow. *Academy of Management Journal, 56*(1). doi: 10.5465/amj.2013.4001

Latif, I. A., Mohamed, Z., Sharifuddin, J., Abdullah, A. M., & Ismail, M. M. (2014). A comparative analysis of global halal certification requirements. *Journal of Food Products Marketing, 20*(sup1), 85–101.

Latif, M. A. (2020). Halal international standards and certification. In Y. R. Al-Teinaz, S. Spear & I. H. A. Abd El-Rahim (Eds.), *The halal food handbook* (pp. 205–226). Wiley.

Latour, B., & Woolgar, S. (1986). *Laboratory life: The construction of scientific facts.* Princeton University Press.

Lauth, H. J. (2004). Formal and informal institutions: On structuring their mutual co-existence. *Romanian Journal of Political Science, 4*(1), 67–89.

Lavandoski, J., Albino Silva, J., & Vargas-Sánchez, A. (2014). *Institutional theory in tourism studies: Evidence and future directions* (No. 2014–3). CIEO-Research Centre for Spatial and Organizational Dynamics, University of Algarve.

Lawton, T., Rajwani, T., & Doh, J. (2013). The antecedents of political capabilities: A study of ownership, cross-border activity and organisation at legacy airlines in a deregulatory context. *International Business Review, 22*(1), 228–242.

Levitsky, S., & Murillo, M. V. (2009). Variation in institutional strength. *Annual Review of Political Science, 12*, 115–133.

Lewis, D. E. (2002). The politics of agency termination: Confronting the myth of agency immortality. *The Journal of Politics, 64*(1), 89–107.

Liasidou, S. (2019). Understanding tourism policy development: A documentary analysis. *Journal of Policy Research in Tourism, Leisure and Events, 11*(1), 70–93.

Lipset, S. M. (1959). Some social requisites of democracy: Economic development and political legitimacy. *American Political Science Review, 53*(1), 69–105.

Loconto, A., & Fouilleux, E. (2014). Politics of private regulation: ISEAL and the shaping of transnational sustainability governance. *Regulation & Governance, 8*(2), 166–185.

Loi, K. I., Lei, W. S., & Lourenço, F. (2020). Understanding the reactions of government and gaming concessionaires on COVID-19 through the neo-institutional theory–The case of Macao. *International Journal of Hospitality Management.* doi: 10.1016/j.ijhm.2020.102755

Lorenz-Meyer, D. (2004). Addressing the politics of location: Strategies in feminist epistemology and their relevance to research undertaken from a feminist perspective. In S. Štrbánová, I. H. Stamhuis, & K. Mojsejová (Eds.), *Women scholars and institutions, Vol. 13b* (pp. 783–805). Research Centre for History of Sciences and Humanities.

Lowi, T. J. (1979). *The end of liberalism: The second Republic of the United States* (2nd ed.). Norton.

Luo, X., Wang, D., & Zhang, J. (2017). Whose call to answer: Institutional complexity and firms' CSR reporting. *Academy of Management Journal, 60*(1), 321–344.

Luo, Y., & Zhang, H. (2016). Emerging market MNEs: Qualitative review and theoretical directions. *Journal of International Management, 22*(4), 333–350.

Lv, Z., & Xu, T. (2017). A panel data quantile regression analysis of the impact of corruption on tourism. *Current Issues in Tourism, 20*(6), 603–616.

MacCarthaigh, M. (2012). Politics, policy preferences and the evolution of Irish bureaucracy: A framework for analysis. *Irish Political Studies, 27*(1), 23–47.

Macdonald, T. (2008). What's so special about states? Liberal legitimacy in a globalising world. *Political Studies, 56*(3), 544–465.

Macridis, R. C. (1968). Comparative politics and the study of government: The search for focus. *Comparative Politics, 1*(1), 79–90.

Majone, G. (1980). The uses of policy analysis. In G. Raven (Ed.), *Policy studies review annual*, Vol. 4 (pp. 161–180). SAGE.

Majone, G. (1981). Policies as theories. In I. L. Horowitz (Ed.), *Policy studies review annual*, Vol. 5 (pp. 15–26). SAGE.

Malesky, E., & Taussig, M. (2017). The danger of not listening to firms: Government responsiveness and the goal of regulatory compliance. *Academy of Management Journal, 60*(5), 1741–1770.

Mann, S. (2016). *Reflective practice and reflexivity in research processes.* Palgrave MacMillan.

Marano, V,, & Kostova, T. (2016). Unpacking the institutional complexity in adoption of CSR practices in multinational enterprises. *Journal of Management Studies, 53*(1), 28–54.

March, J. G., & Olsen, J. P. (1984). The new institutionalism: Organizational factors in political life. *American Political Science Review, 78*(3), 734–749.

Marshall, C., & Rossman, G. B. (2010). *Designing qualitative research* (5th ed.). SAGE.

Mattsson, L. G., & Salmi, A. (2013). The changing role of personal networks during Russian transformation: Challenges for Russian management. *Journal of Business & Industrial Marketing, 28*(3), 190–200.

Maurer, J. G. (1971). *Readings in organization theory: Open-system approaches.* Random House.

McCarthy, B. (2012). From fishing and factories to cultural tourism: The role of social entrepreneurs in the construction of a new institutional field. *Entrepreneurship & Regional Development, 24*(3–4), 259–282.

McDonough, P., Barnes, S. H., & Pina, A. L. (1986). The growth of democratic legitimacy in Spain. *American Political Science Review, 80*(3), 735–760.

McPherson, C. M., & Sauder, M. (2013). Logics in action managing institutional complexity in a drug court. *Administrative Science Quarterly, 58*(2), 165–196.

Mehmetoglu, M., & Altinay, L. (2006). Examination of grounded theory analysis with an application to hospitality research. *International Journal of Hospitality Management, 25*(1), 12–33.

Mehta, A., Goldstein, S. D., & Makary, M. A. (2017). Global trends in center accreditation by the Joint Commission International: Growing patient implications for international medical and surgical care. *Journal of Travel Medicine, 24*(5). doi: 10.1093/jtm/tax048

Mensah, I., & Blankson, E. J. (2013). Determinants of hotels' environmental performance: Evidence from the hotel industry in Accra, Ghana. *Journal of Sustainable Tourism, 21*(8), 1212–1231.

Meyer, J. W. (2008). Reflections on institutional theories of organisations. In R. Greenwood, C. Oliver, T. B. Lawrence & R. E. Meyer (Eds.), *The SAGE handbook of organisational institutionalism* (pp. 788–809). SAGE.

Meyer, J. W., & Rowan, B. (1977). Institutionalized organisations: Formal structure as myth and ceremony. *American Journal of Sociology, 83*(2), 340–363.

Meyer, J. W., & Scott, W. R. (1983). *Organisational environments: Ritual and rationality.* SAGE.

Meyer, J. W., Scott, W. R., & Strang, D. (1987). Centralization, fragmentation, and school district complexity. *Administrative Science Quarterly, 32*(2), 186–201.

Meyer, R. E., & Höllerer, M. A. (2014). Does institutional theory need redirecting? *Journal of Management Studies, 51*(7), 1221–1233.

Meyer, R. E., & Höllerer, M. A. (2016). Laying a smoke screen: Ambiguity and neutralization as strategic responses to intra-institutional complexity. *Strategic Organization, 14*(94), 373–406.

Ming, Y., & Liu, N. (2020). Political uncertainty in the tourism industry: Evidence from China's anti-corruption campaign. *Current Issues in Tourism.* doi: 10.1080/13683500.2020.1852195

Morgan, G. (1986). *Images of organization.* SAGE.

Morrish, S. C., & Earl, A. (2020). Networks, institutional environment and firm internationalization. *Journal of Business & Industrial Marketing,* https://doi.org/10.1108/JBIM-05-2019-0230

Mulaj, K. (2011). The problematic legitimacy of international-led statebuilding: Challenges of uniting international and local interests in post-conflict Kosovo. *Contemporary Politics, 17*(3), 241–256.

Munir, K. A. (2015). A loss of power in institutional theory. *Journal of Management Inquiry, 24*(1), 90–92.

Murphy, K., & Hurst, D. (2020). Coalition to pursue power to block deals such as Victoria's belt and road agreement with China. *The Guardian,* 26 August, https://www.theguardian.com/australia-news/2020/aug/26/coalition-to-pursue-power-to-block-deals-such-as-victorias-belt-and-road-agreement-with-china

Murtha, T. P., & Lenway, S. A. (1994). Country capabilities and the strategic state: How national political institutions affect multinational corporations' strategies. *Strategic Management Journal, 15*(2), 113–129.

Muthuri, J. N., & Gilbert, V. (2011). An institutional analysis of corporate social responsibility in Kenya. *Journal of Business Ethics, 98*(3), 467–483.

Ng, A. W., & Tavitiyaman, P. (2020). Corporate social responsibility and sustainability initiatives of multinational hotel corporations. In W. Leal Filho, P. Borges de Brito, & F. Frankenberger (Eds.), *International business, trade and institutional sustainability* (pp. 3–15). Springer.

North, D. C. (1990). *Institutions, institutional change and economic performance.* Cambridge University Press.

North, D. C. (1991). Institutions. *Journal of Economic Perspectives, 5*(1), 97–112.

North, D. C., & Weingast, B. R. (1989). Constitutions and commitment: The evolution of institutions governing public choice in seventeenth-century England. *The Journal of Economic History, 49*(4), 803–832.

Nunkoo, R., Ramkissoon, H., & Gursoy, D. (2012). Public trust in tourism institutions. *Annals of Tourism Research, 39*(3), 1538–1564.

O'Brien, A. (2010). Beyond policy-making: Institutional regimes, the state and policy implementation in the Irish case. *Current Issues in Tourism, 13*(6), 563–577.

O'Kane, R. H. T. (1993). Against legitimacy. *Political Studies,* 41(3), 471–487.

Oliver, C. (1991). Strategic responses to institutional processes. *Academy of Management Review, 16*(1), 145–179.

Ouyang, Z., Wei, W., & Chi, C. G. (2019). Environment management in the hotel industry: Does institutional environment matter? *International Journal of Hospitality Management, 77,* 353–364.

Pache, A. C., & Santos, F. (2010). When worlds collide: The international dynamics of organisational responses to conflicting institutional demands. *Academy of Management Review, 35*(3), 455–476.

Palmer, A. (1996). Linking external and internal relationship building in networks of public and private sector organizations: A case study. *International Journal of Public Sector Management, 9*(3), 51–60.

Palthe, J. (2014). Regulative, normative, and cognitive elements of organisations: Implications for managing change. *Management and Organisational Studies, 1*(2), 59–66.

Parker, L. D., & Chung, L. H. (2018). Structuring social and environmental management control and accountability. *Accounting, Auditing & Accountability Journal, 31*(3), 993–1023.

Parsons, T. (1960). *Structure and process in modern societies.* Free Press.

Patel, A. M., Xavier, R. J., & Broom, G. (2005). Toward a model of organizational legitimacy in public relations theory and practice. In J. Nussbaum (Ed.), *International communication association conference* (pp. 1–22). International Communication Association.

Paul, J., & Feliciano-Cestero, M. M. (2020). Five decades of research on foreign direct investment by MNEs: An overview and research agenda. *Journal of Business Research.* doi: 10.1016/j.jbusres.2020.04.017

Peng, M. W., Wang, D. Y. L., & Jiang, Y. (2008). An institution-based view of international business strategy: A focus on emerging economies. *Journal of International Business Studies, 39*(5), 920–936.

Perrow, C. (1986). *Complex organizations: A critical essay* (3rd ed.). Random House.

Peters, B. G. (2001). *Institutional theory in political science: The "new institutionalism"*. Continuum.

Peters, B. G. (2012). *Institutional theory in political science. The new institutionalism* (3rd ed.). Continuum.

Peters, G. B., & Hogwood, B. W. (1988). Births, deaths and marriages: Organizational change in the US. Federal Bureaucracy. *The American Review of Public Administration, 18*(2), 119–133.

Peters, S., Font, X., & Bonilla-Priego, M. J. (2020). Why organizations join voluntary sustainable tourism associations: Implications for membership and sustainability monitoring systems. *International Journal of Tourism Research, 22*(3), 325–335.

Pfarrer, M. D., Decelles, K. A., Smith, K. G., & Taylor, M. S. (2008). After the fall: Reintegrating the corrupt organization. *Academy of Management Review, 33*(3), 730–749.

Piekkari, R., Plakoyiannaki, E., & Welch, C. (2010). "Good" case research in industrial marketing: Insights from research practice. *Industrial Marketing Management, 39*(1), 109–117.

Piekkari, R., Welch, C., & Paavilainen, E. (2009). The case study as disciplinary convention: Evidence from international business journals. *Organizational Research Methods, 12*(3), 567–589.

Pierre, J. (Ed.). (2000a). *Debating governance: Authenticity, steering and democracy*. Oxford University Press.

Pierre, J. (2000b). Introduction: Understanding governance. In J. Pierre (Ed.) *Debating governance: Authenticity, steering and democracy* (pp. 1–12). Oxford University Press.

Pierre, J. (2009). Reinventing governance, reinventing democracy? *Policy & Politics, 37*(4), 591–609.

Pierre, J., & Peters, B. G. (2000). *Governance, politics and the state*. St. Martin's Press.

Pierre, J., & Peters, B. G. (2005). *Governing complex societies: Trajectories and scenarios*. Palgrave.

Pierson, P. (2000). Increasing returns, path dependence, and the study of politics. *American Political Science Review, 94*(2), 251–267.

Pierson, P. (2004). *Politics in time: History, institutions and social analysis*. Princeton University Press.

Pike, S., & Page, S. (2014). Destination marketing organizations and destination marketing: A narrative analysis of literature. *Tourism Management, 41*, 202–227.

Popper, K. (1978). *Three worlds, the Tanner Lecture on human values*, delivered at the University of Michigan, 7 April. http://www.tannerlectures.utah.edu/lectures /documents/popper80.pdf

Poprawe, M. (2015). A panel data analysis of the effect of corruption on tourism. *Applied Economics, 47*(23), 2399–2412.

Poulis, K., & Poulis, E. (2016). Problematizing fit and survival: Transforming the law of requisite variety through complexity misalignment. *Academy of Management Review, 41*(3), 503–527.

Powell, W. W., & DiMaggio, P. J. (Eds.). (1991). *The new institutionalism in organizational analysis*. University of Chicago Press.

Prakash, A. (2000). Responsible care: An assessment. *Business and Society, 39*(2), 183–209.

Presenza, A., Del Chiappa, G., & Sheehan, L. (2013). Residents' engagement and local tourism governance in maturing beach destinations. Evidence from an Italian case study. *Journal of Destination Marketing & Management, 2*(1), 22–30.

Pressman, J. L., & Wildavsky, A. B. (1973). *Implementation: How great expectations in Washington are dashed in Oakland; Or, why it's amazing that federal programs work at all, this being a saga of the Economic Development Administration as told by two sympathetic observers who seek to build morals on a foundation of ruined hopes*. University of California Press.

Puffer, S. M., McCarthy, D. J., & Jaeger, A. M. (2016). Institution building and institutional voids: Can Poland's experience inform Russia and Brazil? *International Journal of Emerging Markets, 11*(1), 18–41.

Quintens, L., & Matthyssens, P. (2010). Involving the process dimensions of time in case-based research. *Industrial Marketing Management, 39*(1), 91–99.

Raaijmakers, A. G., Vermeulen, P. A., Meeus, M. T., & Zietsma, C. (2015). I need time! Exploring pathways to compliance under institutional complexity. *Academy of Management Journal, 58*(1), 85–110.

Ragin, C. C. (1992). "Casing" and the process of social inquiry. In C. C. Ragin & H. S. Becker (Eds.), *What is a case? Exploring the foundations of social inquiry* (pp. 217–226). Cambridge University Press.

Ramus, T., Vaccaro, A., & Brusoni, S. (2016). Institutional complexity in turbulent times: Formalization, collaboration, and the emergence of blended logics. *Academy of Management Journal, 60*(4), 1253–1284.

Rao, H. (1994). The social construction of reputation: Certification contests, legitimation, and the survival of organisations in the American automobile industry: 1895–1912. *Strategic Management Journal, 15*(1), 29–44.

Raynard, M. (2016). Deconstructing complexity: Configurations of institutional complexity and structural hybridity. *Strategic Organization, 14*(4), 310–335.

Razak, N. H. A., Hall, C. M., & Prayag, G. (2020). Understanding halal hospitality. In C. M. Hall & G. Prayag (Eds.), *The Routledge handbook of halal hospitality and Islamic tourism* (pp. 21–52). Routledge.

Regenstein, J. M., Riaz, M. N., Chaudry, M., & Regenstein, C. E. (2014). The halal food industry. In M. K. Hassan & M. K. Lewis (Eds.), *Handbook on Islam and economic life* (pp. 175–194). Edward Elgar.

Reid, H. (2020). Unlike Trump, Biden believes in climate change – and his nominees prove it. *CNN*, 18 December. https://edition.cnn.com/2020/12/18/opinions/b iden-nominees-bold-climate-action-reid/index.html

Remondino, M., Penco, L., & Profumo, G. (2019). Negative events in the cruise tourism industry: The role of corporate responsibility and reputation in information diffusion. *Tourism in Marine Environments, 14*(1–2), 61–87.

Rhodes, R. A. W. (1997). *Understanding governance: Policy networks, governance, reflexivity and accountability*. Open University Press.

Riaz, M. N., & Chaudry, M. M. (2004). *Halal food production*. CRC Press.

Riensche, M., Castillo, A., García-Frapolli, E., Moreno-Casasola, P., & Tello-Díaz, C. (2019). Private over public interests in regional tourism governance: A case study in Costalegre, Mexico. *Sustainability, 11*(6), 1760.

Riker, W. H. (1980). Implications from the disequilibrium of majority rule for the study of institutions. *American Political Science Review, 74*(2), 432–447.

Riker, W. H. (1982). *Liberalism against populism: A confrontation between the theory of democracy and the theory of social choice*. Freeman.

Robson, M. (2008). Interviewing the Australian business elite: Let's get down to business. In T. Hays & R. Hussain (Eds.), *Bridging the gap between ideas and doing research* (pp. 151–163). University of New England.

Rodriguez, I., Williams, A. M., & Hall, C. M. (2014). Tourism innovation policy: Implementation and outcomes. *Annals of Tourism Research, 49*, 76–93.

Roth, K., & Kostova, T. (2003). Organisational coping with institutional upheaval in transition economies. *Journal of World Business, 38*(4), 314–330.

Rothschild, M. L. (1999). Carrots, sticks, and promises: A conceptual framework for the management of public health and social issue behaviors. *Journal of Marketing, 63*(4), 24–37.

Rothstein, B. (1998). Political institutions – An overview. In R. E. Goodin, & H-D. Klingemann (Eds.), *A new handbook of political science* (pp. 133–166). Oxford University Press.

Rottig, D. (2016). Institutions and emerging markets: Effects and implications for multinational corporations. *International Journal of Emerging Markets, 11*(1), 2–17.

Roxas, B., & Chadee, D. (2013). Effects of formal institutions on the performance of the tourism sector in the Philippines: The mediating role of entrepreneurial orientation. *Tourism Management, 37*, 1–12.

Roy, H., Hall, C. M., & Ballantine, P. W. (2017). Trust in local food networks: The role of trust among tourism stakeholders and their impacts in purchasing decisions. *Journal of Destination Marketing & Management, 6*(4), 309–317.

Ruhanen, L., & Whitford, M. (2018). Racism as an inhibitor to the organisational legitimacy of Indigenous tourism businesses in Australia. *Current Issues in Tourism, 21*(15), 1728–1742.

Sæþórsdóttir, A. D., & Hall, C. M. (2021). Visitor satisfaction in wilderness in times of overtourism: A longitudinal study. *Journal of Sustainable Tourism, 29*(1), 123–141.

Saka-Helmhout, A. (2020). Institutional agency by MNEs: A review and future research agenda. *Journal of International Management*. doi: 10.1016/j.intman.2020.100743

Saka-Helmhout, A., Deeg, R., & Greenwood, R. (2016). The MNE as a challenge to institutional theory: Key concepts, recent developments and empirical evidence. *Journal of Management Studies, 53*(1), 1–11.

Samkin, G., & Schneider, A. (2010). Accountability, narrative reporting and legitimation. *Accounting, Auditing & Accountability Journal, 23*(2), 256–289.

Saz-Carranza, A., & Longo, F. (2012). Managing competing institutional logics in public–private joint ventures. *Public Management Review, 14*(3), 331–357.

Scholz, J. T., & Wang, C. L. (2006). Cooptation or transformation? Local policy networks and federal regulatory enforcement. *American Journal of Political Science, 50*(1), 81–97.

Scholz, J. T., & Wei, F. H. (1986). Regulatory enforcement in a federalist system. *American Political Science Review, 80*(4), 1249–1270.

Scott, D., Hall, C. M., & Gössling, S. (2016). A report on the Paris Climate Change Agreement and its implications for tourism: Why we will always have Paris. *Journal of Sustainable Tourism, 24*(7), 933–948.

Scott, W. R. (1987). The adolescence of institutional theory. *Administrative Science Quarterly, 32*(4), 493–511.

Scott, W. R. (1995). *Institutions and organisations: Ideas and interests.* SAGE.

Scott, W. R. (2001). *Institutions and organisations: Ideas and interests* (2nd ed.). SAGE.

Scott, W. R. (2005). Institutional theory: Contributing to a theoretical research program. In K. G. Smith & M. A. Hitt (Eds.), *Great minds in management: The process of theory development* (pp. 460–484). Oxford University Press.

Scott, W. R. (2008). *Institutions and organisations: Ideas and interests* (3rd ed.). SAGE.

Scott, W. R. (2014). *Institutions and organization: Ideas, interests, and identities* (4th ed.). SAGE.

Selin, S. (1994). Collaborative alliances: New interorganizational forms in tourism. *Journal of Travel & Tourism Marketing, 2*(2–3), 217–227.

Selznick, P. (1957). *Leadership in administration: A sociological interpretation.* Harper & Row.

Seyfi, S., & Hall, C. M. (2020). *Tourism, sanctions and boycotts.* Routledge.

Seyfi, S., Hall, C. M., & Shabani, B. (2020). COVID-19 and international travel restrictions: The geopolitics of health and tourism. *Tourism Geographies.* doi: 10.1080/14616688.2020.1833972

Shaheer, I., Carr, N., & Insch, A. (2019). What are the reasons behind tourism boycotts? *Anatolia, 30*(2), 294–296.

Shaheer, I., Insch, A., & Carr, N. (2018). Tourism destination boycotts–are they becoming a standard practice? *Tourism Recreation Research, 43*(1), 129–132.

Sharma, S. (2000). Managerial interpretations and organizational context as predictors of corporate choice of environmental strategy. *Academy of Management Journal, 43*(4), 681–697.

Shipilov, A. (2012). Strategic multiplexity. *Strategic Organization, 10*(3), 215–222.

Shove, E. (2010). Beyond the ABC: Climate change policy and theories of social change. *Environment and Planning. Part A, 42*(6), 1273–1285.

Simons, T., Vermeulen, P. A., & Knoben, J. (2016). There's no beer without a smoke: Community cohesion and neighboring communities' effects on organizational resistance to antismoking regulations in the Dutch hospitality industry. *Academy of Management Journal, 59*(2), 545–578.

Smith, K. (2006). Problematising power relations in "elite" interviews. *Geoforum*, *37*(4), 643–653.

Smith, T. V. (1951). Power: Its ubiquity and legitimacy. *American Political Science Review*, *45*(3), 693–702.

Soares, A. L. V., Mendes-Filho, L., & Gretzel, U. (2020). Technology adoption in hotels: Applying institutional theory to tourism. *Tourism Review*. doi: 10.1108/TR-05-2019-0153

Spencer, J. W., & Gomez, C. (2011). MNEs and corruption: The impact of national institutions and subsidiary strategy. *Strategic Management Journal*, *32*(3), 280–300.

Studdert, D. M., Hall, M. A., & Mello, M. M. (2020). Partitioning the curve – Interstate travel restrictions during the COVID-19 pandemic. *New England Journal of Medicine*, *383*(13), e83.

Suchman, M. C. (1995). Managing legitimacy: Strategic and institutional approaches. *Academy of Management Review*, *20*(3), 571–610.

Suddaby, R., & Greenwood, R. (2005). Rhetorical strategies of legitimacy. *Administrative Science Quarterly*, *50*(1), 35–67.

Suddaby, R., Bitektine, A., & Haack, P. (2017). Legitimacy. *Academy of Management Annals*, *11*(1), 451–478.

Suharko, S., Khoiriati, S. D., Krisnajaya, I., & Dinarto, D. (2018). Institutional conformance of Halal certification organisation in Halal tourism industry: The cases of Indonesia and Thailand. *Tourism*, *66*(3), 334–348.

Thaler, R. H., & Sunstein, C. R. (2008). *Nudge: Improving decisions about health, wealth and happiness.* Yale University Press.

Theingi, T., Theingi, H., & Purchase, S. (2017). Cross-border remittance between emerging economies: An institutional perspective. *Journal of Business & Industrial Marketing*, *32*(6), 786–800.

Thomas, J. R. (2014). Shades of green: A critical assessment of greenwashing in social and environmental business performance reports. *Journal for International Business and Entrepreneurship Development*, *7*(3), 245–252.

Thornton, P. H. (2002). The rise of the corporation in a craft industry: Conflict and conformity in institutional logics. *Academy of Management Journal*, *45*(1), 81–101.

Thornton, P. H., & Ocasio, W. (1999). Institutional logics and the historical contingency of power in organizations: Executive succession in the higher education publishing industry, 1958–1990. *American Journal of Sociology*, *105*(3), 801–843.

Thornton, P. H., Ocasio, W., & Lounsbury, M. (2012). *The institutional logics perspective: A new approach to culture, structure, and process.* Oxford University Press.

Tolbert, P. S., & Zucker, L. G. (1999). The institutionalization of institutional theory. In S. Clegg & A. Hardy (Eds.), *Studying organization. Theory & method* (pp. 169–184). SAGE.

Tost, L. P. (2011). An integrative model of legitimacy judgments. *Academy of Management Review*, *36*(4), 686–710.

Treib, O., Bähr, H., & Falkner, G. (2007). Modes of governance: Towards a conceptual clarification. *Journal of European Public Policy*, *14*(1), 1–20.

Triggle, N. (2013). Healthy lifestyles: Is a hug, shove, nudge or smack best? *BBC News Health*, 17 February. http://www.bbc.co.uk/news/health-21593335

Tsai, K. S. (2006). Adaptive informal institutions and endogenous institutional change in China. *World Politics*, *59*(1), 116–141.

Tsai, K. S. (2016). Adaptive informal institutions. In T. Fioretos, T. G. Falleti & A. Sheingate (Eds.), *The Oxford handbook of historical institutionalism* (pp. 270–288). Oxford University Press.

Unwin, T. (1992). *The place of geography*. Longman.

Usmani, M., Davison, J., & Napier, C. J. (2020). The production of stand-alone sustainability reports: Visual impression management, legitimacy and "functional stupidity". *Accounting Forum*, *44*(4), 315–343.

Veblen, T. (1909). The limitations of marginal utility. *Journal of Political Economy*, *17*(9), 620–636.

Veblen, T. (1919). The intellectual pre-eminence of Jews in modern Europe. *Political Science Quarterly*, *34*(1), 33–42.

Vestrum, I., Rasmussen, E., & Carter, S. (2017). How nascent community enterprises build legitimacy in internal and external environments. *Regional Studies*, *51*(11), 1721–1734.

Voronov, M., & Weber, K. (2016). The heart of institutions: Emotional competence and institutional actorhood. *Academy of Management Review*, *41*(3), 456–478.

Walters, G., & Tacon, R. (2018). The "codification" of governance in the non-profit sport sector in the UK. *European Sport Management Quarterly*, *18*(4), 482–500.

Wang, C., Dai, S., Xu, H., & Li, X. (2018). The impact of the institutional environment on the geographic diversification of Chinese tourism firms. *Journal of China Tourism Research*, *14*(3), 334–353.

Wang, C., Kafouros, M., Yi, J., Hong, J., & Ganotakis, P. (2020). The role of government affiliation in explaining firm innovativeness and profitability in emerging countries: Evidence from China. *Journal of World Business*, *53*. doi: 10.1016/j.jwb.2019.101047

Wang, D. T., Gu, F. F., Tse, D. K., & Yim, C. K. B. (2013). When does FDI matter? The roles of local institutions and ethnic origins of FDI. *International Business Review*, *22*(2), 450–465.

Webb, J. W., Ireland, R. D., Hitt, M. A., Kistruck, G. M., & Tihanyi, L. (2011). Where is the opportunity without the customer? An integration of marketing activities, the entrepreneurship process, and institutional theory. *Journal of the Academy of Marketing Science*, *39*(4), 537–554.

Weber, M. (1947). *The theory of social and economic organisation*. Free Press.

Webster, C., & Ivanov, S. (2016). Political ideologies as shapers of future tourism development. *Journal of Tourism Futures*, *2*(2), 109–124.

Weerakkody, V., Dwivedi, Y. K., & Irani, Z. (2009). The diffusion and use of institutional theory: A cross-disciplinary longitudinal literature survey. *Journal of Information Technology*, *24*(4), 354–368.

Welch, C., Piekkari, R., Plakoyiannaki, E., & Paavilainen-Mäntymäki, E. (2011). Theorising from case studies: Towards a pluralist future for international business research. *Journal of International Business Studies*, *42*(5), 740–762.

Williamson, O. E. (1975). *Markets and hierarchies: Analysis and antitrust implications*. Free Press.

Williamson, O. E. (1985). *The economic institutions of capitalism*. Free Press.

Williamson, O. E. (1991). Comparative economic organisation: The analysis of discrete structural alternatives. *Administrative Science Quarterly*, *36*(2), 269–296.

Wilson, W. (1898). *The state: Elements of historical and practical politics*. D.C. Heath.

Windsor, D. (2019). Influencing MNC strategies for managing corruption and favouritism in Pacific Asia countries: A multiple-theory configurational perspective. *Asia Pacific Business Review*, *25*(4), 501–533.

Xiao, H., & Smith, S. L. (2006). Case studies in tourism research: A state-of-the-art analysis. *Tourism Management*, *27*(5), 738–749.

Xu, D., & Shenkar, O. (2002). Note: Institutional distance and the multinational enterprise. *Academy of Management Review*, *27*(4), 608–618.

Yang, I. C. M. (2020). A journey of hope: An institutional perspective of Japanese outbound reproductive tourism. *Current Issues in Tourism*, *23*(1), 52–67.

Yang, J., & Rhee, J. H. (2020). CSR disclosure against boycotts: Evidence from Korea. *Asian Business & Management*, *19*, 311–343.

Yang, Y. L., Lee, S., & Kim, S. (2018). Locus of legitimacy and startup resource acquisition strategies. *Asia Pacific Journal of Innovation and Entrepreneurship*, *12*(1), 32–44.

Yang, Z., & Su, C. (2014). Institutional theory in business marketing: A conceptual framework and future directions. *Industrial Marketing Management*, *43*(5), 721–725.

Yasarata, M., Altinay, L., Burns, P., & Okumus, F. (2010). Politics and sustainable tourism development—Can they co-exist? Voices from North Cyprus. *Tourism Management*, *31*(3), 345–356.

Yee, A. S. (2004). Cross-national concepts in supranational governance: State-society relations and EU-policy making. *Governance*, *17*(4), 487–524.

Yin, R. (2003). *Case study research: Design and methods* (3rd ed). SAGE.

Yüksel, A., Yüksel, F., & Culha, O. (2012). Ministers' statements: A policy implementation instrument for sustainable tourism? *Journal of Sustainable Tourism*, *20*(4), 513–532.

Zahra, A. L. (2010). A historical analysis of tourism policy implementation by local government. *Journal of Tourism History*, *2*(2), 83–98.

Zapata Campos, M. J., Hall, C. M., & Backlund, S. (2018). Can MNCs promote more inclusive tourism? Apollo tour operator's sustainability work. *Tourism Geographies*, *20*(4), 630–652.

Zapata, M. J., & Hall, C. M. (2012). Public–private collaboration in the tourism sector: Balancing legitimacy and effectiveness in local tourism partnerships. The

Spanish case. *Journal of Policy Research in Tourism, Leisure and Events, 4*(1), 61–83.

Zelditch, M. (2001). Processes of legitimation: Recent developments and new directions. *Social Psychology Quarterly, 64*(1), 4–17.

Zeppel, H. (2012). Collaborative governance for low-carbon tourism: Climate change initiatives by Australian tourism agencies. *Current Issues in Tourism, 15*(7), 603–626.

Zhang, M., & Merchant, H. (2020). A causal analysis of the role of institutions and organizational proficiencies on the innovation capability of Chinese SMEs. *International Business Review, 29*(2). doi: 10.1016/j.ibusrev.2019.101638

Zheng, Q., Luo, Y., & Maksimov, V. (2015). Achieving legitimacy through corporate social responsibility: The case of emerging economy firms. *Journal of World Business, 50*(3), 389–403.

Zhu, Q., Cordeiro, J., & Sarkis, J. (2013). Institutional pressures, dynamic capabilities and environmental management systems: Investigating the ISO 9000–environmental management system implementation linkage. *Journal of Environmental Management, 114*, 232–242.

Zimmerman, M. A., & Zeitz, G. J. (2002). Beyond survival: Achieving new venture growth by building legitimacy. *Academy of Management Review, 27*(3), 414–431.

Index

For Product Safety Concerns and Information please contact our EU
representative GPSR@taylorandfrancis.com
Taylor & Francis Verlag GmbH, Kaufingerstraße 24, 80331 München, Germany

www.ingramcontent.com/pod-product-compliance
Lightning Source LLC
Chambersburg PA
CBHW061747270326
41928CB00011B/2403